J R D Campbe

LARGS

Through the Centuries

Published by Largs & District Historical Society

BY THE SAME AUTHOR:-

Millport and the Cumbraes - A History and Guide.

Clyde Coast Smuggling.

The Cumbrae Circles — Outer and Inner.

"LARGS — THROUGH THE AGES"

First published in Great Britain in 1995 by
Largs & District Historical Society,
Kirkgate House, Manse Court, Largs, KA30 8AW.

ISBN 0 9502751 3 1

The Society acknowledges with thanks the financial contributions by Ayrshire Enterprise, Cunninghame District Council and Miss Louisa McKissock's Trust towards the cost of publishing this book.

British Library Cataloguing in Publication Data. A catalogue record for this book is available from the British Library.

Cover design by Jacqui Logan

Computer Typeset and printed by
Largs Printing Company, 120 Main Street, Largs, Ayrshire.

PREFACE

When created in 1876, the Police Burgh of Largs extended over lands which had been part of burghs of barony set up by charters granted in 1595, 1629, and again in 1631. Ultimately these were interlocking — a most unusual situation. What might have lain behind this had always intrigued me — especially as the 1629 charter was granted to an individual with no apparent local connections — so I set out to discover how this might have arisen.

Using pointers given to me by Mr Nigel Tranter, I have been able to arrive at what I am sure is considerably less than the whole picture; but, however inadequate, it is probably sufficient to indicate what may well have been the relative scenario.

The associated researches also opened up other tempting avenues, some of which I could not resist following up. In turn, these explorations introduced me to many people who had a specialised knowledge both of the locality and events that had affected it. I have listed many of these, but there are others who helped me immeasurably in the course of conversation. To all of these I offer my very sincere thanks, as without their help this small volume could not have been produced.

The contents are intended to give an outline of some of the events which have affected Largs over the centuries with particular reference to the property developments of Victorian times. I only hope the reading of it may prove as interesting to native, incomer, and visitor, as its preparation has been to me.

J R D Campbell.

September, 1995

Fig. No 1. Part of Plan of Brisbane Estate in 1805. From a drawing by John Patton.
(Reproduced by kind permission of the Keeper of the Records of Scotland from RHP 558.)

CHAPTER I

WHAT HAS HAPPENED IN LARGS

The derivation of place names is usually a great source of controversy, but in the case of Largs there seems to be little doubt that the origin of the name lies in the Gaelic "Leargs". This can be translated into English as "the plain", or as "the slope facing the sea". Both of these interpretations seem applicable.

The area has gone through various stages of development since pre-historical times. The missionaries who came to convert the heathen to Christianity, were followed in turn by first the Romans and then the Normans. One of the Norman families ("de Calchou" which was later corrupted to "Kelso") established themselves near Manse Court in the centre of the town; and the other ("de Boyuile" which later became "Boyle") near what is now Kelburn Castle.

With "nobility" in control, some method had to be found for them to receive rents in cash as well as in kind, so local markets were set up. Thereafter the town became in turn a small industrial town, a place of residence for the very rich, a holiday resort, and a place to live in retirement or to bring up a family.

Up to the end of the Victorian era there appears to have been two main stages in the town's evolution. In this chapter we will follow the historical events involved, and then in the next two chapters see where these events have left their mark on the town.

The town's nineteenth century prosperity sprang from the pier, and that is as good a reason as any for using it as an imaginary grandstand from which to look back over the ages. We shall take it both as the starting point of our tours covered in the following chapters, and also as a viewpoint from which to "stand and stare" at the truly magnificent panorama spread out before us.

Continuously populated since at least 3,000 BC, or about 5,000 years ago, little is known of the town's very early inhabitants, but they have left us a legacy of Neolithic graves, Bronze Age cists, and Iron Age forts. There are also remains of a Roman military road in the hills behind the town. This ran from the Irvine area to somewhere near Greenock.

Soon after the arrival of Columba on Iona in 563 AD, Christian missionaries arrived in Scotland from Ireland, bringing with them the Celtic (as opposed to the Roman) discipline of Christianity. The first conventional place of worship in Largs stood in the old graveyard just behind Manse Court. This would certainly have been built on the site of a monk's cell.

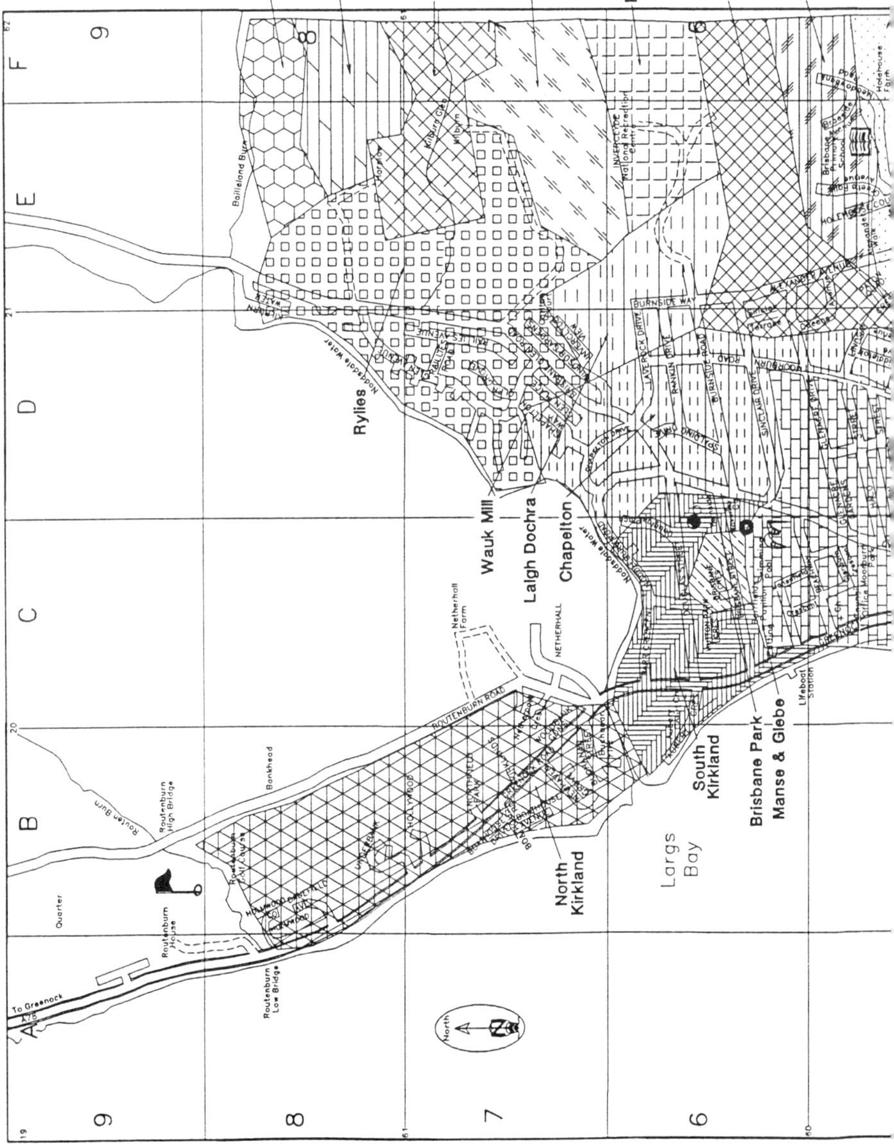

Fig. 2. Plan showing relative positions of 1805 town and 1990 street layout.

Notes

1 1800 AD features are indicated in bold type

2 The various hatchings indicate approximate areas of places indicated not only on map in fig.1 but also in other sources.

3 Reproduced by kind Permission of Nicolson Maps Largs

Fig. 3 Plan showing relative positions of 1811 town and 1990 street layout.

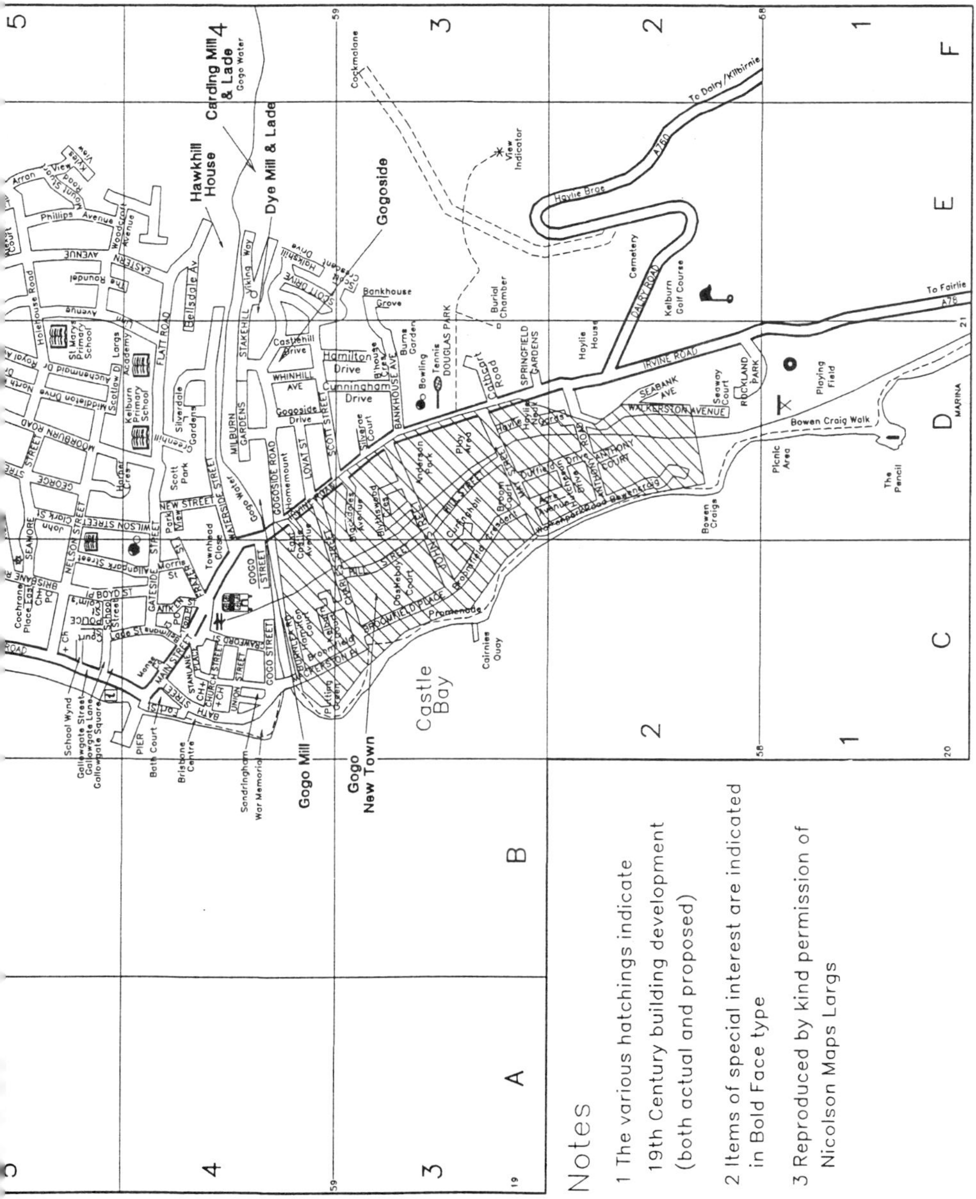

Notes

1 The various hatchings indicate 19th Century building development (both actual and proposed)

2 Items of special interest are indicated in Bold Face type

3 Reproduced by kind permission of Nicolson Maps Largs

In 1263 the Norsemen brought a fleet to Largs with the intention of forcing the Scottish Crown to recognise Norse authority over the western seaboard of Scotland. This expedition failed because of the equinoctial storms, and to a lesser extent the waiting Scots army. Most of the army had come over the hill from Kilbirnie, but, as we will see later, there were also some locals in the force. The Battle of Largs effectively put an end to Viking occupation of the Scottish islands.

Governments always need money, and one of the methods of raising revenue used in the middle ages was to make a levy or "cess" on places where (especially foreign) goods were bought and sold, and where manufacturing was carried on.

To allow these levies to be easily collected, it was laid down that trade should only take place at authorised markets. Initially these were to be held in Royal burghs. Irvine was the Royal Burgh nearest to Largs, and so claimed the right to all trade arising from there. Not that they obtained this right without a fight. Ayr, the slightly older Burgh had also claimed that privilege, but the matter was put beyond any doubt by the Irvine Confirmation Charter of 1372 which decided that Largs fell within Irvine's area for trading purposes.

These centralised markets presented traders with practical difficulties, and many local unapproved markets sprang up to the detriment of those in the Royal Burghs. With ready access to sea-borne traffic, it was only natural that one such market came to be held regularly in Largs. This began to affect trade at Irvine, and in 1538 the Burgesses there formally complained to the Crown about what was happening. The dispute rumbled on, and then in 1595 the Brisbanes petitioned for the grant of a Charter for a Burgh of Barony. This type of charter had been introduced to help smaller communities who were suffering as a result of Royal burgh monopolies, and gave them the right to hold their own smaller markets.

Probably out of spite, in the same year as that happened, Irvine Town Council disenfranchised all "out of town" burgesses, a move which would, of course, affect those from Largs.

Burgesses, it should be explained, were people authorised to carry on a trade, or to buy and sell within the burgh. Usually, but not always, these burgesses were expected to live within the town and to build a house on a toft which they had to acquire there. (A toft was a strip of land usually facing on to the main street where markets were held)

As is not unknown in the world of politics, be it at a national or a local level, principles did not prevail for very long in the face of expediency, so it is not altogether surprising to find that by 1670 out-of-town burgesses were again being appointed in Irvine, including Jas Brisbane Jr of Bishoptoun. Nor again in 1709, when the Town Council needed funds, that they should welcome a loan of 500 merks from the Earl of Glasgow, who somehow at the same time became Provost there. Similarly, in 1727, we find amongst the burgesses a Professor of Greek at Edinburgh, an army officer, a merchant in Arran, a minister in Dunoon, and a merchant in “Langcaster”.

What is also surprising, if from another viewpoint, is that in 1794, the Kirk Session of Largs had apparently possessed sufficient surplus funds to make a loan (amount unspecified) to the same Town Council.

The first Norman family to have settled near Largs were known as de Calchou, later to become Kelso. At the time of the first petition for burghal status the current laird was Archibald Kelso who might have been expected to apply for such a charter, but he seems to have been more interested in politics than in commerce, as, prior to succeeding to the title in 1578, he had been involved in the Battle of Langside (1568) where he was taken prisoner. Later, and more seriously, he was involved in the Gowrie Conspiracy in 1600.

As a result of this last episode he lost his lands.

Against this background, and the fact that before this happened he had attended the Scottish Parliament on at least six occasions, it is easy to see what interested him most. Presumably to avoid any problems these factors might present, the Brisbanes, who were related to the Kelsos by marriage, seem to have stepped in and lodged the 1595 petition which was granted for the “Newtown of Gogo” — but no mention of Largs.

In the latter part of his reign James VI and I (1567-1625) had included Sir William Alexander of Menstrie in his select band of courtiers, but, apart from granting him a charter to found a colony in Nova Scotia, had not given him any office of real note — strange as it may seem the bond between them seems to have been based on their mutual love of poetry — but in 1626, the year after his accession, Charles I appointed Sir William to be Secretary of State for Scotland. The latter soon noted Largs had no burghal status and in 1627, the year after his appointment, he created Largs an approved port for trading with Ireland (this would enhance its commercial value). The next move was made in 1629 when he took a grant of burghal status for the town in his own name.

We will never know the full story, but it is reasonable to assume that some form of settlement had to be effected in his favour before he allowed the formation of a combined burgh of Largs and Gogo in 1631 in the name of the Brisbanes. This Charter granted power to hold four fairs annually, and weekly markets in the church-yard on Sundays. A copy can be found in the Largs Museum. Amongst the lands listed as being within the Burgh, were B(K)illingcraig, Gogoside, Muirburn, Hangandheuche and Largsmure.

James VI had used various methods to raise money. One scheme was to sell “monopolies” to anyone prepared to buy them, and in 1596 the Bishop of Brechin

Fig. 4. Busy pier in 1930s showing numbers of passengers travelling by steamer. (From the Largs and District Historical Society Collection.)

Fig. 5. Pier in 1930s showing signal box to control steamers waiting to get into pier. (From the Largs and District Historical Society Collection.)

was granted a Crown Charter which allowed him to tax all boats fishing for herring between the Pentland Firth and the Mull of Galloway. The Bishop was a nephew of the Earl of Argyll, and was only twelve years old, so it seems more than likely he was just a "front" for the Earl himself.

Collection of the tax was delegated to the Town Clerk of Glasgow, one of whose minions counted the boats working out of Largs, Skelmorlie, Rothesay and Cumbrae and found these totalled 122.

The next event of considerable economic significance to the area was the arrival of a Revenue Cutter sent to try to reduce the amount of smuggling. This arrived in 1634 and was stationed at Great Cumbrae where the Boyles of Kelburn had considerable lands. It seems less than coincidental that in the same year a pier was built at "Kelburne Fute" on the land of the "Laird of Kelburn", and was mainly paid for by the magistrates of Glasgow. This location was, of course, just opposite the Kelburn lands on Cumbrae.

In the circumstances too, it is perhaps not wholly surprising to find that in 1684 John Boyle of Kelburn and a partner had paid £28,000 Scots, or about £2,500 Sterling, for the right to collect all the Customs dues in Scotland.

The pier at Kelburn was in use until about 1885, when it was removed to make way for the railway, and remains can still be traced on the sea shore between Largs Marina and the NATO pier in Fairlie.

Before its construction, and without any other facilities available, cattle and horses coming to the various fairs and markets held at Largs would be unloaded directly on to the shingle at the mouth of the Gogo. These came from Argyll and the islands and as the traffic increased this method became impracticable, so a wharf was constructed there to make things easier.

In the latter part of the 18th century the weavers were reasonably prosperous. From woollen goods, they progressed first to the production of linen and then to "Paisley" shawls. Traces of the processes involved can be found in Brisbane Glen where remains of flax "retting" or rotting pits and of what was possibly a wauk mill can be seen. Also there was a wauk or fulling mill on the Noddle Burn shown on the map of 1805 (fig. 1). The name of the "retting" or rotting burn survives in "Routenburn", and records of the various water mills operating in Gogoside are detailed in Chapter III. Up to the end of the wars with France in 1813 there were at least 400 weavers operating in the town, but from then on the trade went into a decline which proved to be terminal. Most had worked in their homes, but there were also some in "shops" housing four or more looms.

It will be noted that on the west side of the (1805) map is an area shown as "town land", which was the common grazing used by weavers and others, whilst the named areas on the east side of the plan may well represent the "ferm touns",

Fig. 6. Early (1891) Largs railway station.(Note the position of Chanty Dyke enclosure in middle of road.)
(From the Largs and District Historical Society Collection.)

about to be converted into single tenant farm units as a result of the agricultural improvements going on at the time. The map in fig. 2 shows how the present town has spread over them, whilst that in fig. 3 demonstrates the approximate area of the present town that was occupied both by the "weavers' town" and the subsequent Victorian developments. Although not shown in this map, the 1761 manse and glebe stood on the so called "town land". The reason for this omission is not known.

Fortunately, the decline in the weaving industry coincided with another development which was to give Largs a steady source of income for nearly two hundred years - the holiday industry. The "healthful craze of sea bathing" had arrived!

So far as Largs was concerned this was ushered in by two events. In 1812 the first commercial steam ship "Comet" appeared on the Clyde, and 1818 saw the first passenger railway journey in Scotland. Although not immediately apparent, these events were to result in Largs going from success to success as a holiday resort up to the end of World War II.

"Comet" had many imitators, which brought more and more visitors to Largs. Since the "flitt" boats used to ferry passengers ashore from them were not only inconvenient, but in some instances downright dangerous, even resulting in a number of mishaps, public meetings were held (there was no Town Council at that time) and money was raised for the construction of a new pier. This came into operation in 1834 and was such a success that only five years later it was reported that the new steamers were bringing as many as 1,000 people a day into Largs. Some idea of what this meant is shown in fig. 4. These passengers came not only from neighbouring island and coastal resorts, they came also from as far away as the Broomielaw in Glasgow. So great were the numbers of vessels involved that a signal box was required to control the queue waiting to get into the pier. (See fig. 5.)

Rail travel came late to Largs (1885) and resulted in the early timber built station shown in fig. 6 (the present format evolved in the 1930s). Luckily this was the only one of many proposals carried out. Today we can appreciate just how fortunate this was, and our good luck can be attributed largely to the efforts of Lord Kelvin of Netherhall, and Mr Scott of Halkshill.

Amongst other possible schemes discussed was a line to have come down the coast from Greenock to a station at the Noddle bridge; one over the hills from Kilmacolm with a terminus at Nelson Street; one direct from Dalry (see fig. 7); one with a circular line linking Largs with both Ayr and Kilmacolm via a mile-long tunnel entered not far from Brisbane House, and having a station at Largs pier — see figs. 8(a) and (b); and yet another to come under the hills direct from

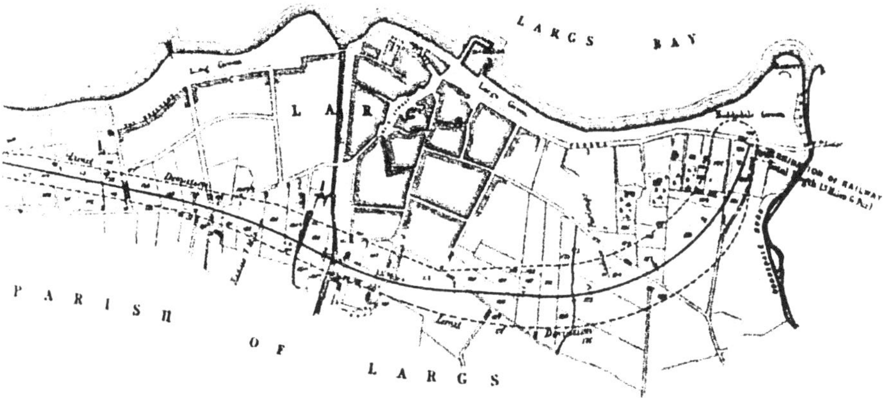

Fig. 7. Plan of proposed line lay out at Largs for rail extension direct from Dalry. (Reproduced by kind permission of the Keeper of Records of Scotland, from RHP 34877).

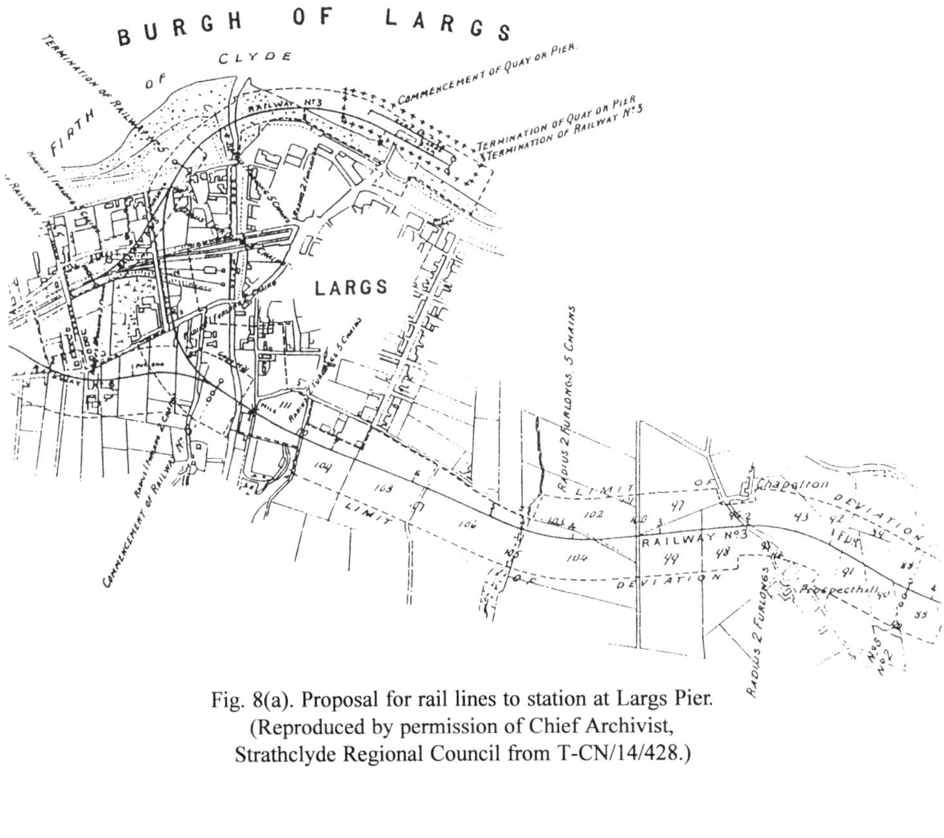

Fig. 8(a). Proposal for rail lines to station at Largs Pier.
(Reproduced by permission of Chief Archivist,
Strathclyde Regional Council from T-CN/14/428.)

Lochwinnoch. Had this latter scheme gone through, the resulting tunnel would have been one of the longest in Europe!

Any one of these schemes would have left us with a far less pleasant town than we have today. In the case of the line from Dalry, the intention was to run the track up from Fairlie just as it does today until it came to the outskirts of the town. There it would have swung further inland crossing Irvine Road near the west end of Scott Street, through Millburn Gardens, over the Gogo, round the east end of Nelson Street, and terminated at Greenock Road, immediately to the north of Hutton Park. As it would have involved raising the level of the road by nineteen feet at one point, the immediate environmental impact would have been considerable and it would also have interfered with the town's development.

The track linking Ayr and Greenock would have broadly followed the same line round the back of the town, and would have had two branch lines to the pier. One, giving access to the south, would have left the line of the present track about John Street, reached the sea front about Charles Street, and then run along the sea front to the pier, whilst the other, giving access to the north, would broadly have followed the line of Charles Street, before joining the main line at the back of the town near Gogoside.

That all of these proposals were considered indicates that the traffic to Largs must have been very profitable indeed. This is perhaps not surprising when the numbers being carried are recalled. By 1905 duplication of trains and outings of parties of 1,300 were quite common, and again in 1907, the first week of the Fair saw trains, running with up to three duplicates, taking away between 600 and 700 passengers daily between 5 am and 8.30 am.

Numbers travelling seemed to have peaked in the period between the two World Wars as at the Easter holiday weekend in 1927 11,820 passengers went through the station; and on one day in 1938 twenty excursion trains were processed. It was little wonder that at times the Largs town water supply had difficulty in keeping the railway engines supplied with water!

In 1877 there had also been proposals to run steam-driven trams between Wemyss Bay, Largs, and Fairlie (see fig. 9). Similar schemes were mooted in 1905 and 1907 when the intention was to use electric or internal-combustion engines instead of steam. To try and head off these challenges, an experimental service of steam railcars was introduced between Largs and Kilwinning. This did not last long — nor did any of the proposed schemes for trams ever come to fruition.

The incoming traffic by steamer was also increasing dramatically. In 1905 one party from the Bethany Hall, Glasgow, coming by steamer numbered 1,200 and by the early 1900s vessels were coming into the pier 3,800 times annually. These were owned by such companies as the Caledonian Steam Packet Co, Glasgow and South West Railway Steamers, Hill & Co, John Wilson, and Buchanan.

Fig. 8(b). Proposal for railway station at Largs Pier c1900.
From collection of Largs and District Historical Society.

The advent of the package holiday industry in the 1960s changed the picture yet again, and, from a tourist viewpoint, the town in the 1990s is more a destination for a day's outing to Nardini's and the seaside, than a residential holiday place.

Business opportunities presented by visitors were naturally very welcome to the town's innkeepers and traders of the late nineteenth century. Nor were they the only ones to benefit from improvements in communications. Ready access to the Glasgow city markets helped fishermen get better and more stable prices for their catches, some taken from boats and some from the salmon nets rigged up along the shore. The fishermen involved were not only local; quite a few working the static nets were "Highlanders" who came to Largs specially for the salmon season.

As elsewhere, the fishing community was a very close one with its own superstitions and customs; some of these customs affected the style of weddings as pictured in fig. 10.

The trade seems to have been reasonably prosperous. Between 1869 and 1900 the number of vessels known to be operating from Fairlie, Cumbrae, Largs and Skelmorlie were as follows:-

	Smacks	*Skiffs or Half Decks*	*Open Boats*	*Total*
Overall Numbers	33	53	145	231
of which those based on Largs were	25	21	101	147

Not all of these boats would be operating at the same time but it is felt the total number registered for the period gives a fairer overall picture of the comparative levels of trade amongst the local communities. For some reason smacks did not seem popular in Largs and most were soon sold on, mainly to Manx fishermen.

Gainfully employed boats meant construction work for local boatyards. In Fairlie both Fife's and Boag's yards flourished; in Largs, McQuiston's yard operated at the mouth of the Gogo; in Skelmorlie, the Tyres had a small yard; and on Cumbrae, Walter Paton had a similar establishment. Nor did the yards build only fishing boats. Large, very impressive racing yachts were turned out; as were smaller racing boats, and row boats for hire. Such was the demand that at one time Fife also had a yard in Rothesay known as the Red Shed.

Up to the end of the Victorian era the town had developed in three phases, but there had also been another scheme which had come to nothing. This was the 1798 proposal for the "New Town of Largs" of which we shall hear more later. (See figs. 11 and 12.)

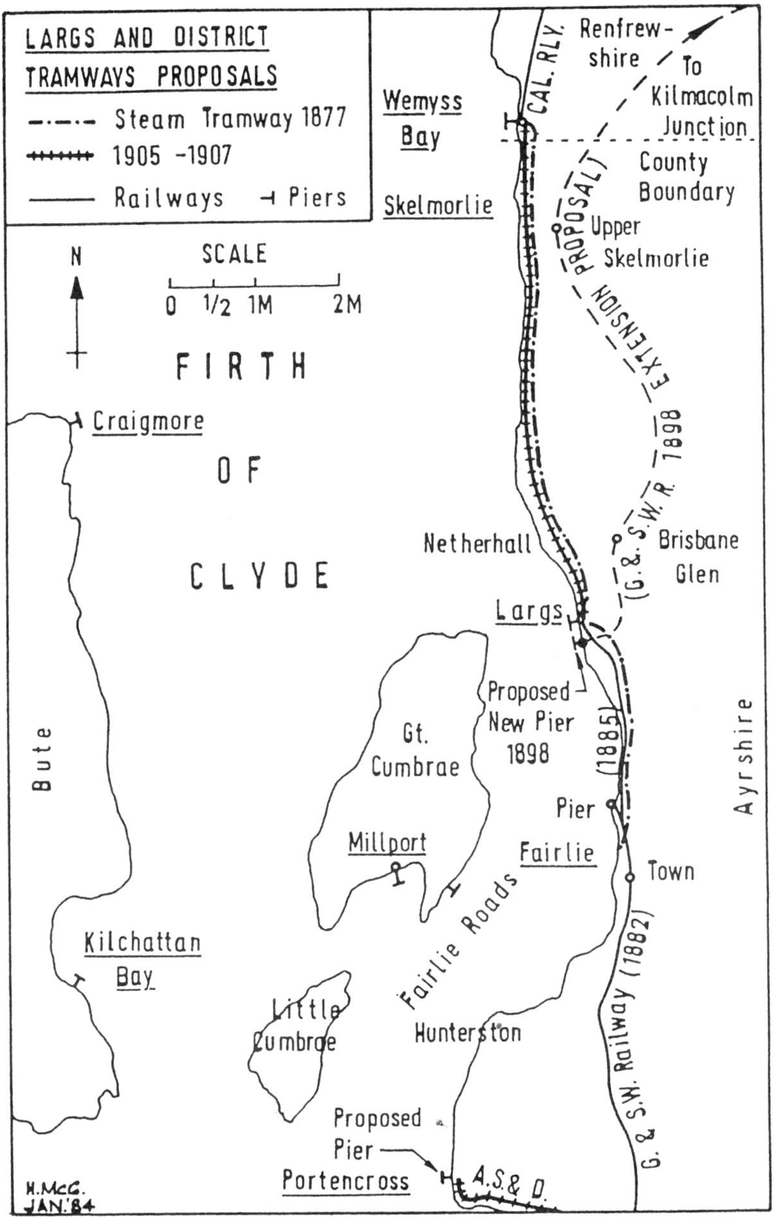

Fig. 9. Map of various proposals for tram services in and around Largs, 1877 - 1907. (Reproduced from "Green Cars to Hurlford" by kind permission of Mr Brian T Deans.)

Unfortunately drawings are not available for all the stages of the various developments, but from those we do have we can see that the existing town shown on the 1798 map was expanded to meet the needs of the increasing weavers' population and resulted in the changes recorded on the 1811 map - fig 13(a). Details of how "Gogo New Town" developed are shown in fig 13 (b), and the intentions for Brisbane New Town of c.1823 are shown in fig. 14. The latter was the final, and the least-successful, proposal.

To help the reader understand what happened, the broad effect of these various stages has been incorporated in overall comparative plans shown in figs. 2 and 3 which help to relate these developments to what we have today. Taken together, the plans reveal that, up to 1798, town buildings were contained in an area approximately bounded on the west by the sea, on the north by Nelson Street, on the east by a line roughly formed by what we now know as Brisbane Road, Allanpark Street and the Gogo Bridge on Irvine Road, and on the south by the Gogo burn; and that the new houses for weavers sprang up between Gateside Street and Nelson Street, and eastwards from Brisbane Road. These comparative plans also show that the "New Town of Gogo" was built on vacant land to the south of the Gogo burn (where fields of broom were to be found), and the "New Town of Brisbane" was intended to start just north of Beachway.

The extensive local railway system enabled those who could afford to do so, to escape both the dirt and disease so prevalent in cities and also the day-to-day stresses of their business. This they did by commuting to a healthier and more pleasant environment of coastal resorts such as Largs where the railway arrived in 1885. Such people usually had profitable businesses, and Largs commuters of the time included owners of concerns carrying household names like Scott, the shipbuilders, Robin's Starch, Donaldson Shipping, Clark's Thread, Buchanan's Toffee etc. Some idea of their life-styles can be obtained from the size of their houses where these still exist - many now divided into flats - but where they have been demolished, photographs of some of them are shown later.

In the circumstances it will be appreciated that new residents were usually very wealthy and with their "chores" taken care of by adequate domestic staff, they were able to devote much time and energy to leisure activities. One of the most important of these was yacht racing as is seen by the detailed reports of the races appearing in the "Wee Paper" during the yachting season, and another was having productive gardens.

Some had massive steam yachts capable of sailing round the world (in 1902 Mr Clark of Curling Hall owned S Y Sybarite which displaced 924 tons); others had very large racing yachts capable of competing with the best in Britain; whilst many more had lug-sails, skiffs and other quite small craft of about nineteen feet

Fig. 10. Scene at fisherman's wedding in late 19th century.
(From collection of Largs and District Historical Society.)

overall. For the owners of large yachts, racing in the waters off Largs was a very serious occupation, and it says much for the standard of sailing they achieved (as well as the social status of the area) that in 1922 the Royal family raced their yacht "Britannia" here. As a result, one of the courses sailed, Largs Bay-Craigmore-Skelmorlie-Mount Stuart, is still known as the "Kings Course". A typical racing scene is shown in fig. 15. This picture, incidentally, also shows how the fishermen sold their catch from small stalls.

World War I put a sudden end to such activities, and, as the list of names on the War Memorial testifies, energies were instead directed to the defence of King and Country.

To administer the large prosperous community it had become, Largs was made a Police burgh in 1876 and the Town Council looked after local affairs of the community from then until 1975 when it was absorbed into Strathclyde Region.

The first steps taken by the newly elected 19th century Commissioners were all positive. A twin screw vessel was chartered to bring slabs from Caithness to pave the sidewalks. They also initiated a system of refuse collection (stable refuse thrown out on to the street was to be uplifted by 9 am daily); provided reservoirs to ensure a better water supply, and a system of underground sewers to replace the open drainage channels. All these measures contributed to the rapidly improving health of the town's residents, a factor on which Dr Caskie was able to comment when he ceased to practise. (He had been the town's medical officer and we shall hear more of this later.)

So much were the early councillors (or commissioners as they were then known) in control of the affairs of the town that by 1902 a newly-erected sea wall and promenade was in place - just in time for the arrival of the Royal yacht "Victoria and Albert" which anchored off Fairlie.

Detailed discussion of the doings of the council are beyond the scope of this volume but a few examples will help to show just how much things have changed since then. One of its functions was to run the burgh court, where "attempting to kiss a young lady" drew a fine of 10/- (50p), whilst, for the theft of £2, a young man with no previous criminal record was given five strokes of the birch. Obviously the Largs outlook was different from that on Cumbrae where, at a similar hearing, two boys were admonished for stealing milk (they were thirsty so they milked one of the cows in a field).

In the early days of the council the system of electing councillors was rather unusual: mock elections for a ward were held before the official polling day, and only the successful candidate from that ballot stood as the official candidate, and so was automatically elected.

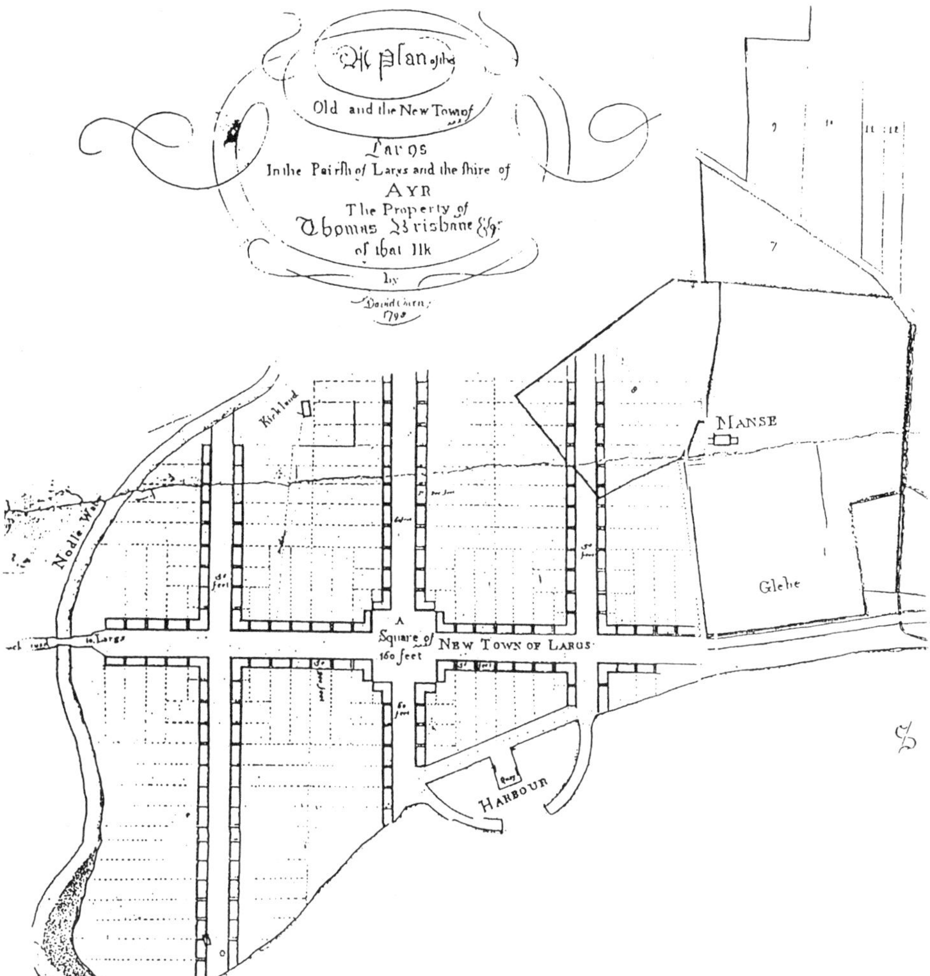

Fig. 11. Plan of proposed Largs New Town 1798 from a plan by David Owen. (Reproduced by permission of Chief Archivist, Strathclyde Regional Council, Reference T-PM 134/113.)

Fig. 12. Map of Largs Town Centre 1798 from a plan by David Owen.
(Reproduced by permission of Chief Archivist, Strathclyde Regional Council,
from reference T-PM 134/113.)

Fig. 13a. 1811 Feu Plan of Largs. As drawn by John Leslie.
(From the Largs and District Historical Society Collection.)

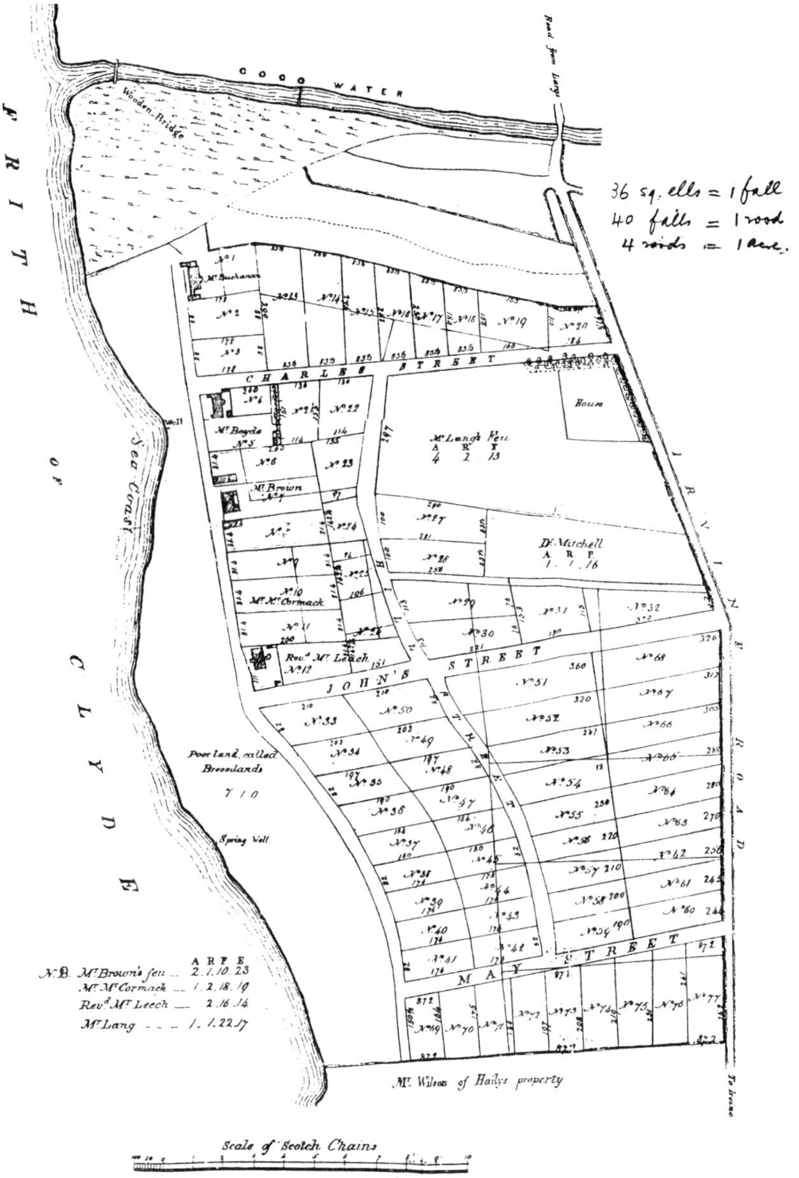

Fig. 13b. 1811 Drawing by John Leslie of feus involved in development of New Town south of Gogo burn. (From collection of Largs and District Historical Society.)

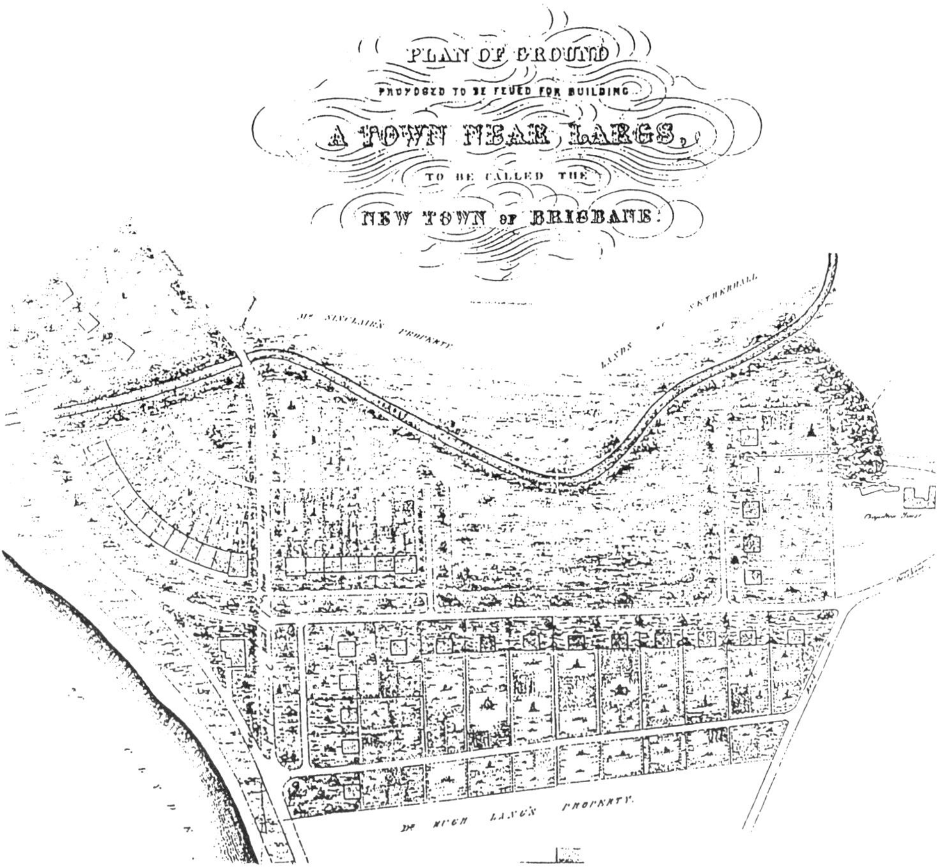

Fig. 14. Plan of Proposed New Town of Brisbane c 1823.
From RHP 42777.

Fig. 15. Typical scene on a yacht race day with fish stalls in foreground.
(Reproduced by kind permission of Arctic Penguin Maritime Centre, Inveraray)

Fig. 16. M V Coruisk and M V Largs ferries at Cumbrae slip with MV Largs "inadvertently" beached.
(Photograph by Mr Walter Kerr, Millport.)

Fig. 17 (a). Aitken Street, Largs c1860 (alias Piper Row, alias Dyet's Close, alias Dyers' Close.)
for comparison with fig 17(b) a century later.
(From collection of Largs & District Historical Society.)

Relations with the town clerk and between councillors were not always cordial. In 1899 the clerk took umbrage at one issue, resigned on the spot, and as the meetings were held in his office, immediately brought all proceedings to a halt by turning out the lights.

One councillor in particular seemed to be almost always at odds with someone, even when he was in the chair as provost. As we will see, most of his efforts were directed at various aspects of slaughterhouses (his own and others) but the municipalisation and subsequent return to private ownership of the gas works also roused his ire.

In 1878 the council had begun to debate the possibility of taking this over, but it was almost ten years later that a settlement figure of £27,990 was accepted. Running it proved more difficult than expected, and by 1901 it was agreed a new company should be formed to take the works over from the burgh. Most of the shareholders and directors of this proposed new company either were councillors or had connections with the council, but for whatever reason the gentleman in question, in spite of the fact that at the time he was actually the provost, tried (unsuccessfully) to set up a rival company for the same purpose.

Details of lifestyles obtained from an examination of old census records are most illuminating. The first example from this source refers to the property known as Northfield at 124 Greenock Road. There, in the 1841 return, the family consisted of Mr J. M. Robertson (aged 60), Miss Mary Robertson (70), Miss Elizabeth Robertson (68), Mr John Robertson (61), and Miss Janet Robertson (50). They were looked after by three female servants and a gardener, who, with his wife and four children lived in a cottage in the grounds. By 1851 there were three elderly Misses Robertson left, looked after by two maids.

The next occupant of the property was the Rev Charles Watson, minister of St John's Free Church in Largs. (His second wife Mary was the sister of the first Lady Kelvin at Netherhall.) By the time of the 1871 census, he, his wife and two sons aged 18 months and 5 months, were being looked after by a cook, a tablemaid, a housemaid, a nursery nurse and a gardener — quite an establishment for a Free Church minister!

The second example is taken from the property known as Danefield at 148 Greenock Road. This was built for Miss Jessie Graham Crum. She knew Largs well as she was a sister of both the first Lady Kelvin of Netherhall, and of the second wife of the Rev Charles Watson of Northfield. She was looked after by a housekeeper, a cook, and three other maids, with a gardener and a coachman for outside duties. Somewhat surprisingly she seems to have "poached" her gardener from the Duke of Northumberland, Alnwick.

By the time this house had been completed in 1885, a lift had been installed, which implies that a supply of electricity was available — a very early example of this.

Fig. 17(b). Aitken Street, Largs c1953. (Alias Piper Row, alias Dyet's Close, alias Dyer's Close.)
For comparison with similar view in fig 17(a) a century earlier.
(From collection of Largs and District Historical Society.)

For whatever reason, some residences at the other end of the town seem to have been predominantly male-bastions. In Curling Hall in 1881 the householder was Mr John Clark who was looked after by three servants; in Broomfield Cottage (now Littleraith), James Stevenson and his cousin were looked after by two servants; and, in Priory Lodge, Alexander Dunlop was looked after by three servants.

It would not be true to say that by 1925 things were back to the situation which had prevailed before World War I, but the frequent comings and goings of the fleet of pleasure steamers gave a superficial aura of prosperity — and thus Largs largely escaped the worst effects of the 1930's depression so apparent in the neighbouring industrial areas.

In 1939 disaster struck again, and Britain was into another war.

Just hours before war was formally declared by Neville Chamberlain, we could have stood on the pier and watched the Home Fleet leaving the Clyde at full speed. This was done so that vessels would be dispersed in the open sea before hostilities began, and so would not emerge as sitting targets for enemy submarines waiting at the mouth of the river.

The Cumbrae marine artist Donald Swan has recorded this scene in a painting that hangs in the Museum of Transport in Glasgow. He was serving on the fleet at the time, and close inspection will reveal a puffer making its way across the river as usual. It was not going to be deflected from its normal course by any Home Fleet!

Because of restricted press coverage of the time, the extent of the contribution made by Largs to the Allies' eventual success in the war is not appreciated, and it is only little-by-little that what had been going on is now becoming public knowledge. Even that can be but a fraction of the whole story.

During this period "locals" could not help but see (and hear) the large numbers of military personnel around the town — in fact many had individual servicemen billeted on them. There were also naval and combined services craft coming and going to the pier, lorries whose contents were carefully screened from the public gaze, and troops undergoing "commando" training which included such activities as jumping into the sea in full kit. The roar of aircraft engines must have been almost continuous as vital, but mundane, routine servicing of seaplanes was done at Barrfields — some of the planes having just returned from operational missions, whilst others had been ferried in from Canada.

The billeting in private homes had some unexpected side-effects. For the adult population there was grief when their "lodgers" did not return from a foray into enemy territory, and there were the usual romances; but for young boys, these paled into insignificance when compared with the glorious opportunities they had of coming in contact with real arms and ammunition. As a result, the schools held periodic amnesties for the return of purloined items!

Fig. 18. Frazer Street, Largs c1870 (Alias Theophilus Close, alias Frazer Close, alias Gas Close).
For comparison with figs. 21 and 22.
(From collection of Largs and District Historical Society.)

What was not seen or fully realised at the time was the part the town played in what has since been described as the greatest exercise in logistical planning the world has ever known. In Largs were situated: the HQ of the First Army; the HQ of Combined Operations; the HQ of Numbers Two and Three Commando; the pay and accounts unit for Combined Operations; the administration unit for the Fleet Air Arm; and more importantly, the planning unit that co-ordinated the strategy for the opening of the Second Front.

Associated with this latter unit, the town had its share of visits from Churchill, Eisenhower, Montgomery and Mountbatten, the latter apparently living aboard his own yacht — while the others came by train.

Some inkling of the scale of these operations can be gained from the number and size of the relative premises involved. This we can grasp in more detail if we follow the walks outlined in Chapters II and III.

Happenings nearer home also affected the town. After the bombing of the Greenock/Port Glasgow area many evacuees came to stay, even if only for a short time.

The year 1945 saw not only the end of hostilities — it also saw the beginning of changes which came slowly at first, but soon accelerated. First came the inauguration of a regular air service between Scotland and Iceland. One of the Catalina flying boats based at Largs was used for this first flight, and took off from the water in front of Barrfields. Whilst the service was not to operate from Largs permanently, it was a portent of what the future held.

Perhaps the best example of the ever-increasing use of modern technology is seen with the arrival of the IBM who set up a factory at Greenock. Initially IBM personnel were located in part of the former torpedo factory, where a staff of 10 manufactured electric typewriters; by 1990 something like 3,000 employees, many of whom were resident in Largs, were producing computers in a purpose-built factory outside Greenock.

The advent of diesel (as opposed to steam) propulsion for ships enabled road vehicles to be carried to the islands and other ferry mainland terminals without their having to be loaded on the ferries by means of a crane, being driven on to it over two planks of wood, or by some similar "Heath Robinson" arrangement. A vessel with side-loading facilities for vehicles was introduced in 1954. Initially this ran from Largs or Fairlie to Arran and Cumbrae on two or three days each week, but the introduction of other similar vessels soon allowed the service to operate daily.

Hovercraft carrying only passengers were also experimented with between 1961 and 1971. Running between Millport, Largs and Rothesay, these proved unsuitable for the prevailing wave patterns.

The need for vehicle ferries now proven, 1971 was to see a fundamental change

Fig. 19. Aeriel view of central Largs c 1953, showing remains of Norman motte (circled). (Reproduced by permission of Hunting Aerofilms Ltd., Gate Studios, Borehamwood, Herts.)

in the pattern of operation. Circular trips in the Clyde estuary were cut out, and only the shortest possible sea crossings from the mainland were serviced. This meant that the only vessels to operate to and from Largs were small ferries running between a newly-constructed landing slip at Largs pier, and a similar slip at the former "Tattie Pier" on Cumbrae.

Whilst this service was intended to operate at frequencies which would meet the needs of the ever-increasing numbers who were commuting to and from the island daily, it was also planned to provide such duplication as was required for tourist traffic at weekends and holiday times; but things did not quite work out like that.

The craft initially used on the route were unsuited to their task, and the preparatory crew training was wholly inadequate. Hundreds of car exhausts were damaged because of inherent vessel design defects, and crew errors led to various problems.

Fig. 16 shows one of these. In this case only one of the vessels was involved: but on another occasion all three vessels on the route found themselves stranded on the Cumbrae slip simultaneously, and, with the tide receding, this blocked all access to the island for several hours. The vessels in question were M V "Coruisk", M V "Broadford" and M V "Largs". Incidentally, it is understood that the last was so renamed by Caledonian MacBrayne to placate the Town Council who were claiming that the vastly increased numbers of vehicles using the new ferries were disrupting local traffic.

Once further experience of the operating needs of the route had been obtained, and purpose-built vessels (partially EEC funded) came into use, the efficiency of the operation improved considerably.

There have been many other changes too. The electrification of the rail service, and an improved roads network, have helped to reduce the journey time to Glasgow to under an hour, and so have encouraged many more to commute to Glasgow daily.

With improvements in technology and modern medicine, more people have additional leisure time available. Many of these do not wish to be involved with gardens, so a larger proportion now resides in flatted developments erected on the sites of former "big hooses".

Such then is the historical background of events which have shaped Largs as it is today. Let us now look at the actual buildings of the town, and thus put into perspective life as it must have been in days past.

Fig. 20. Largs Main Street 1883 showing open sewer running right down main street.
(From collection of Largs and District Historical Society.)

CHAPTER II

A MARKET AND WEAVERS' TOWN

The rapid increase in the number of weavers residing and working in the town came just at the end of the eighteenth century, so the town plan of 1798 (fig. 12) is very definitive of the area covered. Similarly the old photographs of Piper Row - fig. 17(a) - and Frazer Street (fig. 18), before they were modernised, give a very good indication of the state of the buildings in the town at that time.

The former also shows how new tenements were developing in Gateside Street whilst the old town could still be said to be in a decrepit state.

What is also very interesting about the 1798 plan is that it had also included plans for a "New Town of Largs" and although, as we will see, these particular proposals came to nothing, they were an indication of what was to come.

What we will look at now is the state of the town as it developed immediately after the boom in weaving, and also after the steamship came to the fore.

Built in 1834 by the Largs Pier & Harbour Co. Ltd., the Largs pier, from which we start our exploration, remains basically unaltered to this day — although a landing slip has been added in the harbour for the use of ferries running to Cumbrae. The reasons for introducing these roll/on-roll/off vessels have been explained in the previous chapter, but one cannot avoid giving a nostalgic thought to the "weel-kent" paddle steamers of yesteryear, which, with their well-stocked bars and their own accordion bands, linked Largs with piers at Ayr, Arran, Millport, Tarbert, Rothesay, Wemyss Bay to name but a few — now, with the exception of PS Waverley, all gone for ever.

Looking around from the pier, two buildings immediately catch the eye. One is the pleasant appearance of the flats and shops built in 1992 on the site of the former Moorings building. This had itself been built on the site of a cafe sold to the Castlevecci family by a Cornelli Antoria about 1920. The other is the former shepherd's cottage which is such a landmark away up on the hill behind the town. Now a very respectable private dwelling, Cock ma Lane as it is known, has had its day in many ways, including providing shelter for an illicit still found operating there as late as 1908.

The original Moorings, too, had many uses. It was not only used as the restaurant and ballroom for which it was designed. During World War II part of it was used as an overflow Catholic Church; part housed HMS Copra, the Combined Operations Pay and Accounts unit; and in 1960 was again used as a substitute place of worship when the newly-constructed St Mary's Church in Greenock Road became unusable because of a fire.

Fig. 21. Chanty Dyke, Aitken Street, Largs (probable animal pen). Compare with similar view in figs. 18 and 22. (From collection of Largs and District Historical Society.)

The sweeping modern lines of the multi-storey building make it very hard to imagine how the street must have looked in the early 1800s. At that time, one of the single-storey houses in the "Forth" (now Fort Street) was the base for the local Customs and Excise unit established in Largs. Besides providing office space, this also housed the officers' cutlasses and pistols and other weaponry. Details of the surprising extent of their armament, and various incidents in which these Customs Officers were involved, make fascinating and entertaining reading and have been dealt with more fully in the author's "Clyde Coast Smuggling".

An amusement arcade was built to the north east side of the pier in 1955 on a piece of land which the town council had wished to acquire in 1936. Unfortunately, the delays involved in corporate decision-taking allowed another party to step in and buy it. An action brought by the council to have this competing deal set aside was unsuccessful.

Leaving the pier and walking up Main Street, and turning to the left at George Hotel (formerly Brisbane Arms Hotel), we come to Manse Court. Here we find the local museum in Kirkgate House. The building was adapted from a former block of two-storey weavers' cottages. Beside it are the steps that lead into the original kirkyard. For those interested in family history, the museum houses both a computerised data base which has analysed details of interments in the kirkyard between 1823 and 1866, and many old photographs showing named personages of the past.

To the right of the steps are mill-stones quarried from Kaim Hill near Fairlie, whilst to the left of these stairs is a (1901) block of flats, built on the site of the first post-Reformation manse. The latter had been erected around 1600, and, according to the Rev David Baxter, when it was sold to Alexander Frazer, "Wright and Mason" in 1761, it had become rather decrepit. In spite of this unflattering description, the addition of two forestairs enabled the building to be used as a block of "single-ends" for the next century and a half!

The replacement manse was built on ground which at the time (in the late 18th century) was outside the town on the way to Greenock. Just what this looked like we cannot be sure. An old manse was demolished in the 1930s but the architectural features shown in fig. 39 do not seem to fit in with an early eighteenth century structure. The whole area taken up by the manse and its glebe is approximately what is now occupied by Barrfields, Queen's Hotel, Springfield Hotel and the houses in Mansefield Crescent.

Although it is now no longer visible, according to the town plan of 1811 (see fig. 13a) there was a well in the middle of Manse Court. Originally, this might have been a natural spring. If so, the fact that there was just such a nearby spring would have influenced the first missionary in his decision as to where to place his cell. This was because the Welsh/Irish discipline which brought Christianity to Largs

Fig. 22. Gas Tower and west end of Frazer Street, Largs c1950. Compare with similar view in figs. 18 and 21.
(From collection of Largs and District Historical Society.)

laid this down as one of the requirements for the location of a cell. The first missionary arrived not long after Columba settled in Iona in 563 AD and others in his tradition followed. Certainly not all of them came prior to 644 AD, the date of the Synod of Whitby. This was the Synod which decreed that the Celtic church in Scotland would be replaced with that of the Roman tradition. In spite of this decision, many missionaries continued to teach in the Celtic discipline, and seemed to have had a substantial following in Scotland for a further four hundred years. It was only in the time of Malcolm Canmore (1058-93) that the Roman discipline became truly predominant.

Of the Largs pre-Reformation church little is known, but as it was donated to the Bishop of Glasgow in 1191 it must have been built before then, almost certainly on the site of a missionary's cell.

The revenues of this were given to a nunnery at North Berwick in 1199. Looking at the state of communications at the time, the connection with North Berwick seems odd to say the least — especially as the founder of the nunnery was the Earl of Fife. (Because of this some scholars, with whom the author does not agree, argue the deed in question refers to the church at Largo in Fife.) However there is no doubting the authenticity of the transfer charter signed by Joceline, Bishop of Glasgow, with its almost intact Bishop's seal, conveying to the nunnery "ecclesia de Kirkbride de Larges". In view of this and other similar conveyances of Ayrshire-based revenues to the North Berwick nunnery land at Barrebeth (now Craigangillan near Straiton) pre 1200 AD, and the church at Maybole in 1250 — all done at the request of the Earl of Carric (sic) or one of his vassals, it may be safe to assume he had some family connection with it.

To return to the present, Skelmorlie Aisle, which stands in the graveyard, and comes under the control of Historic Scotland, is now all that remains of the old parish church.

Built by Sir Robert Montgomerie of Skelmorlie Castle in 1636 in memory of his wife who had been killed by the kick of a horse at a Largs Fair, the vault below the Aisle contains three coffins; two of lead and one of wood. In the first two lie the bodies of Sir Robert and his wife. The third is occupied by bones found under the floor during restoration work. According to local tradition they are the remains of Sir Hugh Montgomerie, killed at the Battle of Otterburn in 1388.

The ceiling has panels painted with scenes depicting local events and places. One of these may show the 17th century church with the attached aisle. If so, it is the only picture of it. According to an old guidebook, the stones from the old chuch were used to raise the height of the graveyard wall at the time of the "bodysnatchers" scare around 1828.

Three other items in the graveyard are worthy of inspection.

The first is the Brisbane Vault which contains the remains of the Brisbane family, including those of Sir Thomas Makdougall Brisbane, its most prominent member. (The Brisbane River and City of Brisbane in Australia were named in his honour as a result of his sojourn there as Governor General of New South Wales.)

The second feature is the isolated wind-eroded wall standing in front of the Aisle, erected by the Boyles of Kelburn (now Earls of Glasgow) a few years before the building of Skelmorlie Aisle. Some of the design can still be seen.

The third is the crude font of the old church which can be found lying against the wall in one corner of the graveyard.

Behind the Brisbane Vault are remains of a bronze age Beaker Burial Cist which dates from before 1000 BC. Whilst a Christian burial ground may seem an incongruous setting for such an artefact, this was considered the most appropriate location for it when it was removed from its original site in Irvine Road, opposite the top of May Street.

Over the wall on the north side of the small cemetery is a large unkempt and overgrown mound, known locally as the "Gallowhill". This is all that remains of a Norman motte dating from the late 12th or early 13th century, and was probably erected by Roland de Calchou after he married Eva, daughter of Sir Richard de Morville in 1195. Her dowry seems to have consisted of lands at Blackmosse, Halie, Hauginheugh, Dalry, Noddesdale and Armsheugh. The family was later to become "Kelso". Some of this family fought and died at the Battle of Largs.

Public access to the motte is not easy, but neighbouring occupants are often prepared to co-operate with interested visitors. Some idea of what it looks like can be obtained from the aerial photograph shown in fig. 19.

Returning to Manse Court and thence to the Main Street, we pass between a shop on our left and on our right the George Hotel.

The shop and the flats above it were once the surgery and home of Dr Caskie who came to practise medicine in Largs in 1826. Besides being the local doctor he was also the equivalent of the modern Sanitary Inspector and Medical Officer of Health for the town, for which his salary was £5 per annum. Largely as a result of his efforts, improvements were made to the sanitary conditions which helped to contain outbreaks of cholera and typhoid fever which were common when he began his career. He was later to point out that a combination of these steps and the advances made in medical science during his lifetime meant that by the time he retired some fifty years later such diseases had been practically eliminated from the town. It should, of course, also be borne in mind that at the time he came to Largs many of the weavers were on the point of starvation, and so susceptible to all types of infection; and by the time he retired most of the populace were reasonably well fed, and so more capable of resisting disease.

Basically, what he did now seems to us to have been very simple. He instigated a system of open sewers in almost every principal thoroughfare, which being continuously flushed with water from the Gogo burn, washed effluent out into the sea instead of its stagnating and so breeding disease. As can be seen in fig. 20, one of these drains ran down the middle of Main Street which we are now entering. Just how this water was provided we will see later.

So greatly was he appreciated by his patients that, when he retired in 1876, Dr Caskie was presented with a silver Tea and Coffee Service and salver. His bust may be seen in the Museum.

After he ceased to occupy the building, his two sons took it over and ran a pharmacy and a dental practice.

Nor does he seem to have been the first medical practitioner to occupy the area. In 1797 there is a Sasine reference to John King, a surgeon, occupying premises near the entrance to the church at Largs.

The Brisbane Arms, now the George Hotel, was the main coaching inn of the town, and it was also the terminus for a service of horse-drawn 'buses which operated between Largs and Fairlie station during the period between the railway's arrival in Fairlie in 1882 and its coming to Largs in 1885. The old stone hitching posts can still be seen at the front entrance, although the tethering rings are thought to be a relatively modern addition.

As the population of the town grew, so the number of stalls at the local market increased, until there was no longer space for them all in the churchyard where the markets were originally authorised to be held. To resolve the problem, additional places were provided nearby in Main Street, which explains the rather unusual width of the street opposite to the entrance of Manse Court.

Turning left up Main Street, we pass the Royal Bank of Scotland which has occupied this site since the late 1970s. (Completed in 1900, the year the siege of that town was raised, this building was known to older residents as the Mafeking Building.)

If we walk eastwards and take the first road off on our left, what we have entered is Bellman's Close, (one of the town's bellmen lived there for many years), but it has also been known as Manse Close and Kirk Close. On the corner, we pass on our right what was the site of the Post Office until it moved to the first of its positions in Aitken Street and here too had been the original office of the Chamberlain of the Burgh of Largs.

Bellman's Close leads into Lade Street, and here, just next to the cemetery entrance, stood a slaughter house. In the early years of the Town Council this caused much controversy because, although the butcher who owned it was a town councillor, he does not seem to have paid too much attention to the regulations that governed its operation! So much so that, if press reports are to be believed, the effluent (which contained live maggots) flowing from the slaughterhouse turned the churchyard into a "cesspool".

In an attempt to improve matters, it was agreed at one stage that offal would be uplifted by the Council workmen daily, instead of just every alternate day. And all this was going on when, at a different niche in the social spectrum, the local flower show had separate classes for white and black grapes!

Here too is the other entrance to the old churchyard and Skelmorlie Aisle, and in 1880, somewhere about here stood an aerated water factory.

On the same side of Lade Street is what was originally Brisbane Academy. Now called the Stevenson Institute, this was named after James Stevenson of Haylie, who acquired the building from Sir Thomas Brisbane when Brisbane Academy closed in 1893. He converted it into a "Mechanics Institute", with an extensive library intended to meet both the educational and cultural needs of the people of Largs. It is also interesting to recall that a laundry was built on the junction of School Street and Lade Street, and its new chimney stack was blown down in a gale in 1901.

The name "Lade Street" gives cause for speculation as to its origin. Some argue that a lade ran along there to take away water from the open sewers, but it seems more likely that the name has some connection with the family of Lades who were closely associated with the town, many of whom lie in the graveyard. To give some support to this argument there is a Sasine reference to an 1821 transaction with a John and Robert Lade buying a house, yard, and kiln "on the east side of the road leading to the Quay of the Town of Largs".

Turning right into School Street we find a sheltered housing complex alongside the police station and its associated court house. The latter were built in 1871 and 1892 respectively, replacing their more centrally-placed predecessors in Gogo Street, demolished to make room for the railway station.

Over the years, School Street has been occupied by such buildings as Logan's Hall; the Parish School which became the RC Primary School; an RC Church and rectory; Auburn House; and a small tenement.

This church was used by the Roman Catholic congregation until the present church in Greenock Road was opened on 24th June 1962.

Where we turn right into Boyd Street stands the Brisbane Hall, built in 1929 to provide a place of worship for the Plymouth Brethren.

Continuing right along Boyd Street towards the town centre so that we can get to Gateside Street, we come to the business carried on by A H Mackie & Co, which moved here in 1930 from the original premises in Aitken Street, previously.

Piper Row. Founded in 1608 as a blacksmith's business, it is now the last of the three or four which once could be found working in the town.

Incredible as it may seem, this business forged weapons in the 1830s which were intended for use in a proposed Chartist Rebellion. Fortunately this proposal came to nothing.

Over the years, the nature of the blacksmith's work has changed very considerably. Originally hand bellows were used to heat up the fire; these were followed by a gas engine, which in turn was replaced by an electrically operated blower. With the replacement of oxen with horses, horseshoeing came to the fore. Discontinued in 1945, this activity was replaced by light engineering and the making of agricultural implements, and gardening tools.

The figures of Tam o' Shanter and Souter Johnnie on the facade of the building were bought along with the business of Frazer's Smithy in Frazer Street, when the Mackies took it over.

As Gateside Street was originally known as "Weavers' Row", it can be no surprise to learn that this was a part of the town which once housed many weavers. Where we joined this street, we turn right, and then left, into what was formerly known as Pyper (or Piper) Row. Before that it was Diet's (or more probably Dyers') Close, and is now named Aitken Street after the first Provost of Largs. It is a busy thoroughfare at the very heart of the town, but, as will be appreciated by looking at the 1798 plan shown in fig. 11 and the photographs in figs. 17 (a) and (b), taken before and after being widened in 1879, it was a narrow, tortuous road lined by small thatched buildings. The decision to widen the street was not taken lightly. Two years of discussions produced two possible schemes. One involved wiping out the slaughterhouse there, the only one operating in the town in opposition to that owned by one of the councillors. Amongst hints of strange proceedings concerning various properties, it may or may not have been coincidental that this plan was adopted, in spite of the fact that the other plan had as its aim a road which would have run almost straight through from Brisbane Road to Main Street, a facility which would certainly have been appreciated today. Just how easy this would have been, can be seen by comparing the two photographs in question.

The site in Aitken Street occupied by the Post Office from 1927 until 1994 (when it moved about twenty yards along the street) had previously been used as a joiner's business; and Mackie's original smiddy had stood for many years on the corner of Aitken Street and Tron Place, where there is now a pharmacy.

At this corner we turn right into Tron Place. (The "tron", or the town's official scales and weights to check on those used by the market traders, stood about here — possibly near where Woolworths is now.)

Here was located the "Tron Tree", one of the places at which the local weavers gathered when they wanted a blether. Not that they were the only "community" to use it. Traditionally it was also the spot where the local fairies and elves came together in the "wee sma' hours". Because of this, so the story goes, when some-one cut down the tree to spite them, the "little people" had their revenge on the sow belonging to the guilty person, as this was found dead next day.

Arriving back at Main Street, we turn left into the large open area in front of the station, where a family of Hyndmans had a bleaching green. Originally from Inverkip, the family seem to have had connections with the wine trade, both legitimate and otherwise, and in Largs had also occupied property both around the west end of Frazer Street, and in Gogoside. The "green" as such had become superfluous when production of linen ceased towards the end of the eighteenth century, so when, about the same time, more market space was sought for additional traders than could be found lower down the Main Street, it was pressed into use for stalls. (The 1818 population of 2272, practically double that of twenty years previously, naturally attracted more and more traders to the weekly markets.)

It was also used at the fairs. Four annual fairs were approved in the town's charter, the most important of which was "Colm's Day Fair", but apart from the local Historical Society holding a coffee morning somewhere near its official date (the first Tuesday after the 12th June of each year), this is no longer observed.

In the 1880s the area of Hyndman's Green was earmarked for use by tramway services that it was proposed should run from Wemyss Bay to Fairlie and beyond. Perhaps fortunately, none was actually constructed.

The town's tolbooth and the original jail seem to have stood on the edge of the "green", (these should not be confused with the building in Gogo Street used as a jail in the nineteenth century) but no trace of them remains.

The tolbooth was, amongst other things, the centre of management for the old Burgh's affairs, so, with the surplus "green" available, it was the logical collecting point for the feuars' animals. From there it would be easy for the Burgh herdsman to take them each morning to common grazing along Brisbane Road — this was probably that land marked on the 1805 plan in fig. 1 as "toun land" — and to which he would return them each evening. This procedure died away with the enclosure of the common pastures about 1830.

The walled collecting pen, which came to be known as the "Chanty Dyke", was sited in the centre of the area, approximately where the traffic island now stands (see figs. 6 & 21). Later from the same spot, it would have been possible to look up Frazer Street at the far-from-picturesque gas tower (see fig. 22). It is interesting to compare this picture with the very early photograph taken at almost the same angle taken over a century earlier, which appears in fig. 18.

As we walk down Main Street towards the pier, we cross Crawford Street - at one time known as Orr's Close. On the opposite corner is the Jubilee Building bearing the date 1887 and the initials "J W". The story goes that it was built for a ship breaker, John Watson, who in its construction utilised the timber he happened to have handy from a vessel he was breaking up. This was HMS Iron Duke.

On the next corner we come to a pleasant building, built in 1908 to a design by Sir Thomas Washington Browne as a branch of the British Linen Bank. It stands on the former site of Stanlane House, which, for many years, had been the home of the Houstons, one of the fishing families of Largs. When the British Linen Bank merged with the Bank of Scotland in 1971 the office was taken over by a legal firm.

The narrow street that runs down the side of it is currently known as Stanlane Place, but it has been previously known both as Cumbrae Close, and as Haylie Blair Close.

With all the changes that have taken place over the years it is interesting to reflect how the centre of the town on Glasgow Fair today might have compared with Colm's Day - say two hundred years ago.

Today we have the noise and bustle of the traffic, not to mention the exhaust fumes: then there were noises from the animals in their stalls (including the Chanty Dyke), or in the slaughterhouses; the calls of the stall holders and the voices of their customers; the hammering from the two or three smithies and a joiner's shop; but above all we would have had smells! These would have come from animals and their droppings, kilns smoking fish or meat, slaughterhouses, and cesspits of nearby houses. Not that all the animals would be for sale. On Fair days small herds of goats would be brought in to provide instant supplies of milk.

By comparison, the aroma from the distillery would be a welcome relief! Perhaps the "good old days" were not so good after all.

Further down Main Street we turn left into Bath Street. At one time a kiln for smoking fish and meat stood about here. More recently, the corner building on our left, now occupied by a legal firm, has also housed the "King's Arms" pub, a branch of the Union Bank of Scotland with Messrs Eckford and Young as joint agents, a branch of the City Bank, and a dentist's surgery.

At the south end of Bath Street, we see on our right a single-storey building which stands on the site of what was the Earl of Bute's coachhouse. As he had access by sea from Mount Stuart on Bute, the Earl could easily cross to Largs where there was a sheltered haven for his yacht in the small inlet evident in the 1798 map (fig. 12), so the Earl kept a coach here for use when he wished to travel around this part of the mainland — and in particular to his property at Dumfries House near Cumnock. The inlet in question has now been infilled.

This replacement Victorian building was constructed in 1816 to provide both salt-water and vapour baths for those too fearful, or too modest, to face a dip in the

Fig. 23. Lower Gogo Bridge before storm of 1910.
(From collection of Largs and District Historical Society.)

Fig. 24. Gogo Street, Largs, before the 1885 arrival of the railway. The building shown on right of street near bridge was used as jail in 19th century.
(From collection of Largs and District Historical Society.)

sea. A coffee house and circulating library were also available to add to the relaxed, leisurely atmosphere. Its seawards-facing windows look towards the pier, on which much of the past prosperity of the town has depended. Today the north part forms the Green Shutter Tearoom, whilst the rest contains Toc H rooms and a small hall. This has been used for a variety of purposes including meetings of the Plymouth Brethren from 1870 to 1922, and as a local base of TOC H in World War II, and as the local library.

Almost opposite this former Bath House is Clark Memorial Church. Completed in 1892, this building replaced the old Secession church in Waterside Street. The entire cost of the church (which has a seating capacity for over 700) was met by Mr John Clark of Anchor Thread Mills in Paisley. An amateur organist, he liked to slip into the church and entertain friends to recitals on the instrument he had provided; a practice which, according to hearsay, seemed to annoy the church managers. Somewhat unfortunately, they decided to have the locks changed to prevent such occurrences, and in so doing they may well have sacrificed an endowment intended to help with the maintenance costs of the building.

At the time of its construction, the congregations of Clark Memorial and of St Columba's Parish Church vied with each other as to which church would have the taller spire. Clark Memorial has a slight advantage.

The neighbouring building, St John's Church of Scotland, began its life as Largs Free Church, and was later known as St John's United Free Church. The main part was built in 1843, with the spire and Romanesque facade added in 1886. When the Free Church separated from the Parish Church at the Disruption, accommodation for worship was needed in a hurry, so it made sense to erect the basic building to a simple design, with any embellishments added when time and money allowed. (In fact the original part of St. John's was erected in six months.)

Beyond St John's Church, across Union Street, are two blocks of flats known as St John's Court and Sandringham.

St John's, the nearer, originally known as "Seaview", was erected about 1840 by Captain McPherson. Taken over by the YWCA as a holiday home for working girls in 1888, it was redeveloped as flats in 1966. In the course of the conversion two extra floors were added.

Sandringham is the block of flats in red sandstone. This stands partially on the site of the former Relief Church built in 1761, the diminishing congregation of which joined the Burghers in Waterside Street in 1847, allowing it then to be used by the Scottish Episcopal Church before their church was built at Aubery Crescent. The other part of the site was McQuiston's boatyard. Sandringham was built in two phases with the first part completed in 1905 and the second in 1908. The story goes that Mr John Clark had originally intended that his church should be built on this site, but when word of who was involved leaked out, the asking price began to escalate, and Mr Clark lost interest.

On our right we see the memorial to the dead of two World Wars. Erected by public subscription, it was dedicated initially in 1921. The stone-mason was Kellock Brown of Glasgow.

We can also look seawards to where the modern promenade has replaced the wooden wharf so extensively used in the eighteenth and nineteenth centuries, when trade in cattle and other sea-borne items was flourishing. The promenade extending to the pier and known as the Alexandra Parade, was opened in 1902, somewhat later than planned because of the illness of King Edward VII which caused his coronation to be postponed.

Before we turn left into Gogo Street we can pause for a moment, and admire the bridge over the Gogo burn dedicated to the memory of Sir Thomas Brisbane. This was erected in 1911 to replace the original shown in fig. 23 that was washed away in a flood in the previous year.

Proceeding now up Gogo Street we walk alongside the burn before we cross the railway pedestrian bridge. As we do so we should pause at the top and imagine how the view to the north would have been had the space been still occupied, not only by private houses and gardens, but also the old tolbooth. The map contained in fig 8 gives some idea as to how the various gardens ran at that time.

Gogo Street as it was before the arrival of the railway is shown in fig. 24. To the right of the road, facing toward the camera, is what appears to be a Victorian type villa. At the rear of this, however is an older structure used as the town's jail in the nineteenth century. This was all demolished in 1985 to make way for a modern block of flats.

At the end of Gogo Street, turning into Irvine Road, stands the grey sandstone tenement known as "Spencer Buildings", built on the site of the former "Glasgow Hotel". Funds for this (1897) project originated in a legacy inherited by a "local" from an Australian relative.

Over on the other side of the Irvine Road we can see the rather uninteresting Works Depot of the local District Council. Originally used to house the "scaffie cairts" and horses, it was first extended to shelter the Burgh fire engine, and later still was upgraded to provide offices for the Gas Manager and Burgh Surveyor.

About the time these latter improvements were made in 1908, the Council had also considered using the next door dwelling as offices and meeting rooms, but, at the last minute, had second thoughts.

The original Irvine Road bridge over the Gogo at this point was constructed in 1724, but has been widened several times since. When trade was prosperous, weavers used to gather here to "set the world to rights".

We now head back briefly down towards the pier, and turn into the first street on our right, which is Waterside Street.

Before piped water was introduced to the town, one of the wells in this street was supposed to provide the best water for making tea; so whenever visitors were expected in the "Big Hooses", maids were sent to the "Tea Well" (situated roughly where, a garage forecourt now stands) to ensure the tea would be of a sufficiently high quality. One-upmanship is no new thing!

A few yards up the street, the premises now occupied by an antique showroom still leave no doubt as to the building's origin. This was the church erected by the United Session Synod in 1826 as a replacement for an earlier building constructed in 1780 as a meeting place for the burghers. This synod was made up of the reunification of the elements known as the New Licht Burghers and the New Licht Anti Burghers, who had divided in 1747. In its turn this congregation was also joined in 1847 by the congregation of the Relief Church which had stood on part of the site of the flats known as Sandringham.

"Manseburn", the house still standing alongside it to the left, was the manse.

It is not intended here to try and explain the underlying very complex story of the various sects of the Church of Scotland known as the Auld Lichts, the New Lichts, the Burghers and the Anti Burghers. In the interval between its being used as a church and being acquired by its present owners, this building served as a public hall providing a platform for such people as Mrs Pankhurst, the Suffragette leader, and Joe Wesley's Minstrels, as well as acting as a cinema (first The Picture House and then The George).

Prior to the first of these church buildings being available, the burghers had met for worship in a tent which was pitched further up the street near the mound on which stand three pillars. These pillars were erected by Sir Thomas Brisbane in 1809, as "sighting posts" to let him line up accurately the magnetic astronomical instruments in his observatory in Brisbane Glen.

The mound had other uses too. Here the weavers gathered both to chat, and to practise throwing their "clegs" at a target attached to a thorn tree known as the Reformer's Tree. These missiles were originally designed for use in Paisley. There, it should be explained, because of civil unrest over the conditions of the late 18th century, martial law had been imposed from time to time. When this happened, no one could leave their houses. To circumvent this difficulty and still make their point, some of the residents (mainly weavers) determined that their protests against authority still take some tangible form, and so they devised projectiles known as "clegs". Small, easily thrown, dart-like objects, they could, almost literally, be rained down from the upper windows of houses on to the dragoons and their horses in the street below. So far as the Largs weavers were concerned, however, they

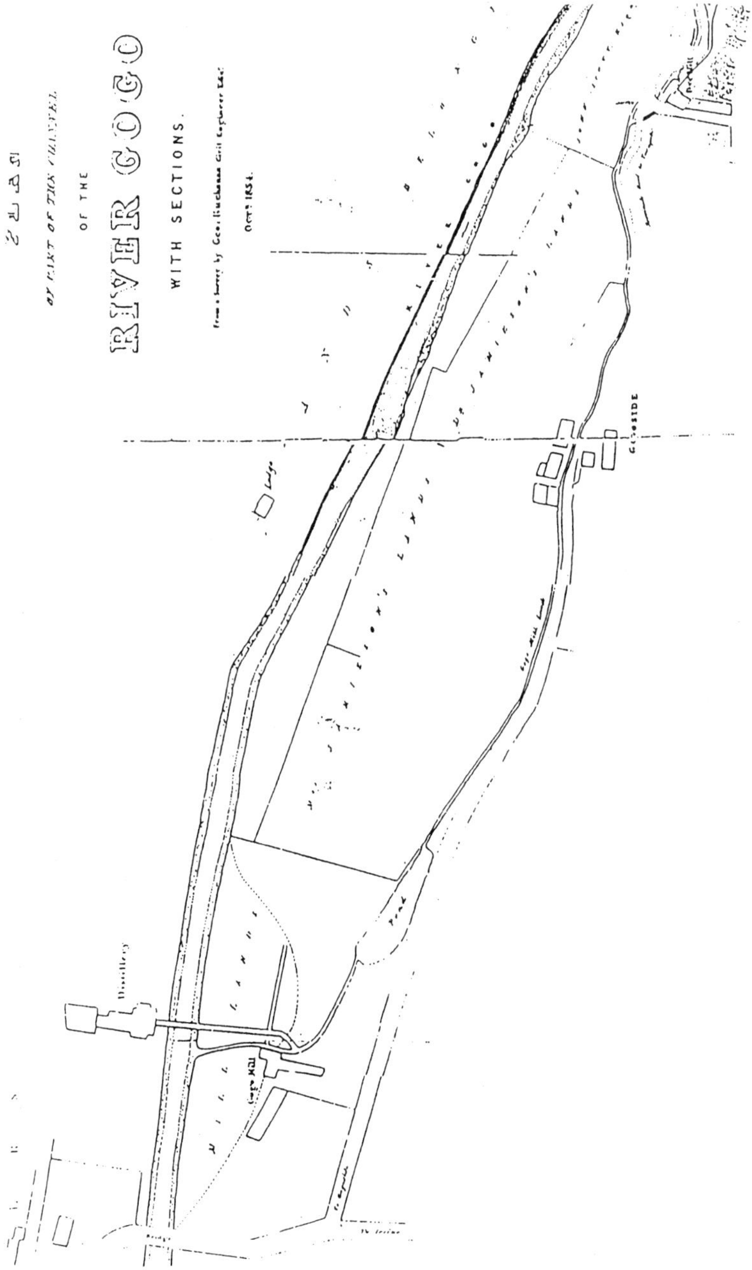

Fig. 25. Plan of 19th century water supply from Gogo burn to distillery, and later to sewers. (Reproduced by kind permission of Keeper of the Records of Scotland, from RHP 12803/3.)

were intended to be used against French forces in the event of a Napoleonic invasion.

Almost opposite here was the site of the town's only distillery, whose water supply came over an aqueduct from the Gogo burn. The first record of this appears in 1788 when John Wilson, maltman, acquired "part of Waterside Croft, called Waterside Faulds". Distilling ceased in the early 1800s because of circumstances outlined in "Clyde Coast Smuggling" published by St Maura Press.

When no longer needed for distilling, the water continued to be fed over the aqueduct to flush out the system of open sewers that had been installed in the principal streets as described above. (See fig. 25.)

At the top of Waterside Street we come to Halkshill House, (called Hawkhill when built in 1815) now owned by the Nardini family. The land on which it stands had been sold in 1810 by Sir Thomas Brisbane to Mr John Scott, shipbuilder of Greenock. What is now the main part of the house was originally meant to be the stables for a new house the Scotts intended to erect on the site of Flatt Farm. Occupied by them as a temporary residence until the planned "big house" could be built for them, the family became so very attached to the adapted stables that they simply had these extended to form the present attractive house, which remained in the Scott family until 1971.

Returning to Irvine Road, before we go down to the pier, we stop to look at the entrance to the very narrow Frazer Street which probably takes its name from the family who had a blacksmith's shop where a pharmacy now stands. Interestingly this is not the first time this practice was followed. The Frazers seem to have acquired the business from a Theophilus Rankin and, in his time the street had been known as "Theophilus' Close" and is referred to as such in a Sasine Register entry. To confuse matters even further,it was also known as "Gas Close", because the Gas Works had been sited there. Fortunately for the appearance of the town, both the works and the gas tower shown in fig. 22 have long since been demolished.

Whilst nominally a blacksmith, Mr Rankin (and/or his son) was obviously a man of parts. The name Theophilus Rankin appears with twelve others on the Poll Tax Roll of 1698. It is also on the Window Tax Rolls of 1749 and 1759 for the parish of Largs, and, from time to time, as a representative of the parish at meetings of various statutory bodies. One of these was of the Supply Commissioners, when, in 1747, the other representative from Largs was a Mr George Paton.

In the circumstances it seems fair to assume there was at least a father and son of the same name.

As we have seen, in the days of the Town Council the operation of the gas plant was always a cause of trouble, and it was probably a great relief when it was nationalised in 1947. The works were then demolished in stages as the gas grid came into effect.

At the east end of Frazer Street, on the south side, are a number of modernised cottages which can give some indication of how the streets in Largs must have looked two hundred years ago when the whole town consisted of such buildings, although as old photographs show, they were not so smart as they are now. At the west end, where it intersects with Aitken Street, the shop that faces down towards the sea, and is now a jeweller's, was occupied by the Hagen family for many years, as electricians and plumbers, and was previously a branch of the Paisley Savings Bank.

Although we have now completed a circuit of the town centre, there is still one part of the original Largs to be looked at. That is the area which is now locally known as the Gallowgate. In the very early days of the town this was the area that would have lain around the original church and Norman motte. Later, as the name implies, it must have been used for hangings. Now access to the motte can only be gained either through the old churchyard or through the adjacent joiner's yard. If the latter, his permission will have to be sought in advance.

To explore the rest of the area, we first of all return to the foot of Main Street, and proceed northwards up the Greenock road. As we do so, we pass on our right a series of shops first occupied just about the time of the opening of the pier. Perhaps it is not surprising that many of them started out as "grog shops" bearing such names as "Earl of Glasgow Arms", "The Weavers Arms", and the "Eagle Inn". In Gallowgate Square is the rather older "Anchor Inn" which dates back to the mid-18th century and is quite a contrast to the red sandstone building in the square which faces seawards, and was constructed in 1913 as the Town Council Chambers and offices. There the administration of the town was carried on until 1936, when the staff and councillors moved to Moorburn House further along Greenock Road.

Sir Walter Scott and his son-in-law, John Gibson Lockhart, lodged in Gallowgate Square when on a visit to the town: here Mr Fleck, a controversial 19th century solicitor, town clerk and councillor, had his office; and here too Dr John Campbell resided and practised medicine for about sixty years.

It was also the location for an establishment run by Mrs Spiers which, for many years, catered for the annual dinner of the Largs Lugsail Club.

Continuing along Gallowgate Street we come to the corner with Nelson Street where we find St Columba's Church of Scotland. The present red sandstone building was opened in 1892, and was the sole official Church of Scotland parish church for Largs until 1929, when the parish was divided. The building it replaced was a smaller church, which had been built on the same site some eighty years earlier.

Impressive architecturally, it has fine stained glass windows some of which were designed by Dr Douglas Strachan who was responsible for the stained glass windows at the War Memorial Shrine in Edinburgh Castle.

As will be evident from the 1798 map (fig. 12), at the time the first church was built on the site, this would have been just outside the limits of the "old town". Buildings began to go up in what is now Nelson Street in the early 19th century, and when excavating the foundations of number 73 Nelson Street, some ancient Bronze Age earthenware burial urns were discovered. Some of these can be seen today in the Glasgow Museums and Art Galleries in Kelvingrove. These houses were intended to house the many weavers who had come into the town in boom times of the early 1800s, but as this trade fell on hard times shortly thereafter, most of the eastwards development in Nelson Street was taken over by the ever-increasing numbers of holiday makers who were providing the town with a welcome additional source of revenue.

In its day this street has housed some famous holidaying families. Probably the two most notable of these were the Burrell family of shipping, and later "Burrell Collection", fame; and the Thomson family, of whom William Thomson was later to become the foremost mathematical physicist of his day. In recognition of this he was made Lord Kelvin. For his retirement he had a new mansion built at Netherhall, in Greenock Road, and whilst this was being done he rented "Auchenean" in Nelson Street, which, now radically altered, forms part of the famous restaurant belonging to the Nardini family.

For the Burrells there are three comparatively simple gravestones in Largs cemetery on the Haylie Brae. Lord Kelvin lies in Westminster Abbey, but his wife is buried in Largs cemetery.

At this point let us go up Nelson Street to the intersection with Boyd Street. About two hundred yards to the left, at the corner of Seamore Street, is the site of the Artillery Drill Hall which was built in 1876, and later used as an office for the Social Security Dept until it was demolished in 1991. To the right, at number 32 Boyd Street, is a two-storey building which was opened in 1852 as a "Female School of Industry", where the emphasis was placed on the girls learning sewing, knitting and baking, although they were also given instruction in the usual academic subjects.

When the pupils were transferred to the newly-opened Largs Public School in 1893, the headmistress of the time, Miss Lyon, made it a formal occasion, and walked her pupils in a crocodile up Nelson Street into the new school in Moorburn Road.

Since taken over by the Parish Council, the former school building has had several uses including being a "Poor House", and a home for the elderly known as "Largs Retreat". It is now the local offices of the Social Work Department.

By the time we reach this point we will have exhausted ourselves physically with all the walking, and mentally by trying to absorb all the details of what we

Fig. 26. Two views of proceedings at 19th century fairs, one of cattle the other of horses. (From collection of Largs and District Historical Society.)

have seen, so it seems only right that we should allow ourselves some form of refreshment. This we can obtain by returning to Nardini's café. Sitting here, it seems incredible that in World War II shelter was provided for refugees from the Greenock Blitz.

Whilst we drink coffee or eat ice cream, we can look out on the part of the foreshore where livestock used to be sold on Fair Day, and, with the aid of the photographs shown in fig. 26, try to imagine the scene.

Because of the sheer numbers of animals to be sold, the lesser merchandise would be on sale in Main Street or Hyndman's Green. Renowned for the quality of the horses and black Highland cattle traded here at the height of its fame in the eighteenth and nineteenth centuries, the annual turnover at the fairs and markets exceeded 2000 cattle alone. Such a large number of animals took up a lot of space, hence the reason for the horses and cattle for sale being lined up along the foreshore from the Noddsdale to the Gogo burns - a distance of approximately 2 kilometres. The animals were from a wide area, mostly coming by sea from the Inner and Outer islands, as well as from Kintyre. To indicate which horses were for sale, red ribbons were tied to their tails.

Moving such a large number of animals to and from the fairs obviously presented transport difficulties, and if neither the pier at "Kelburne Fute" nor the wharf at the mouth of the Gogo was available for unloading, beasts were simply "persuaded" to swim for the shore.

When no fairs were in progress, the sea front was used by the town's fishermen either to display their wares (see fig. 15) or, nearer the mouth of the Gogo, to lay up their boats. These must have been very spectacular sights, because as we will have gathered from Chapter I, between 1850 and 1900, no fewer than 50 boats were based on Largs at any one time.

The foreshore was bought by the Town Council from Miss Florence St. Aubyn Brisbane in 1919 to protect the amenity of the sea front. As a result it will be available for recreational use in perpetuity. On early maps part of this shore is shown as Noddsdale Green, and part as Forth or Largs Green. This latter part is now Fort Street.

Such was the town before the Brisbanes decided to feu off land to the many willing buyers who wished to take advantage of the ever-easier methods of travelling from the cities. Just how this affected Largs we will now consider, whilst at the same time exploring the town's industrial area that was Gogoside.

Fig. 27. Part of old hamlet of Gogoside c 1850.
(From collection of Largs and District Historical Society.)

CHAPTER III

NINETEENTH CENTURY NEW TOWNS

As we have seen, the first mention of a New Town intended for Largs was dated 1798. Conceived before the age of steam, and at a time when the state of the roads left much to be desired, it is difficult to see who would have wished to live in a New Town there which consisted of a formal layout of streets fifty feet wide, built around a formal square with sides measuring one hundred and sixty feet — a concept more appropriate to the west end of Edinburgh or Glasgow than to a rural area such as Largs. Second thoughts obviously prevailed and a scheme providing individual feus was substituted a few years later. As we will see this proved immensely popular.

By the end of the eighteenth century it was just becoming possible for very wealthy individuals who owned well-organised businesses in Greenock, Glasgow, or wherever, to delegate management responsibility to competent staff whilst they themselves lived in Largs or elsewhere to enjoy all the benefits that followed. The Brisbanes saw such residents as a way of improving their financial position, so they changed their line of attack and drew up two other speculative housing schemes designed to attract them.

The first was the development of unproductive scrubland covered with broom, to the south of Largs, which was the "New Town of Gogo"; whilst the second, "Brisbane New Town", consisted of a slightly different proposal for the area to the north.

The first feus in Gogo New Town were granted in 1811 — see fig 13(b) — and this development was immediately successful. Many purchasers took multiple feus on which to build substantial houses, and soon all available land was taken up. Because of delays, mainly caused by legal problems, the second scheme, "Brisbane New Town" came to the market at a time of economic depression, and only a small part of the proposals was carried out.

To try and follow the sequence of events, it seems logical to walk round the main streets of both these developments — again taking the pier as our starting point. Although details have been obtained of some individual houses, for a variety of reasons these may not be quite precise, (for example a full confirmatory search of the Sasines Register has not been possible), but those which are available will still be sufficient to give a fairly accurate picture of life in Largs at that time.

From the pier we proceed up Main Street to the upper bridge over the Gogo burn where we find ourselves in Irvine Road. No one can be sure where the name

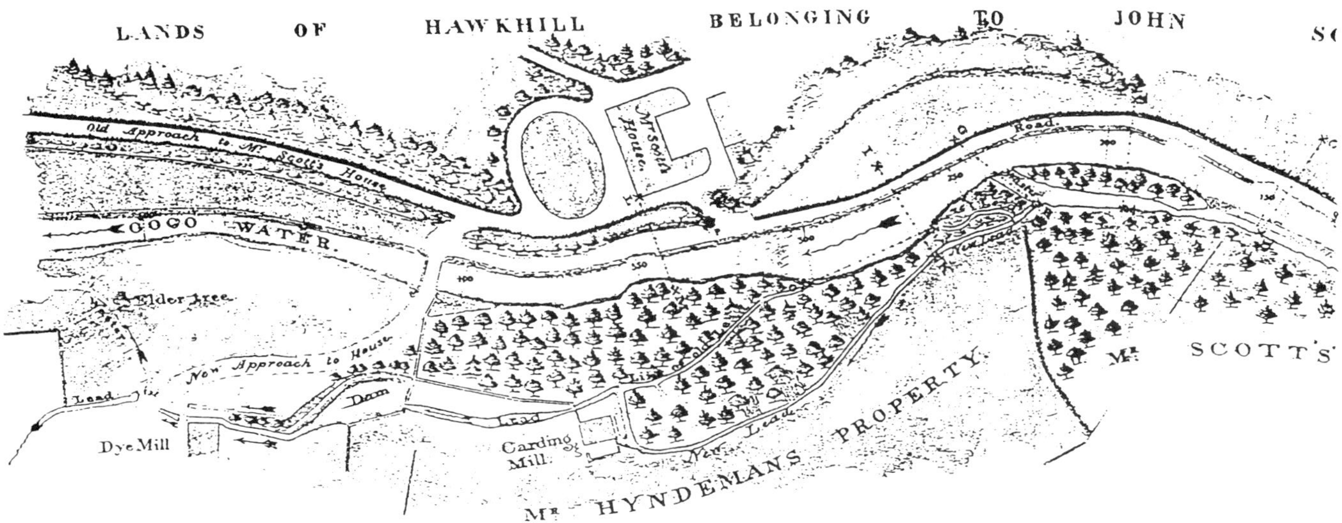

Fig. 28. Plan of 19th century Mill Lades from Gogo burn.
(Reproduced by kind permission of Keeper of Records of Scotland,reference RHP 280/2.)

"Gogo" came from. Usually the stream flows quietly, but heavy rain or melting snow makes the water level rise very rapidly indeed; so much so that at times in the past, simultaneous spates both here and at the Noddle burn at the other end of the town effectively isolated Largs from the rest of the country.

On our left, almost immediately after we have crossed the Gogo, is a building which housed one of the mills which were the mainstay of the small community of Gogoside. Unfortunately this former mill is now a part of business premises, so we can only view it from the front entrance or from Gogoside Road. It seems strange to think that this is all that remains of a thriving separate community that existed for so many years on its own.

Separately referred to in the Burghal Charter of 1631, one of the few surviving photographs of part of it is reproduced in fig. 27. The main function of this community had been to run the mills that served the Largs cottage weaving industry. These had included a lint (flax) mill, a weaving mill, a dye mill, a wool mill, and a carding mill. That there was also a meal mill here goes without saying. In addition, there had also been a fulling, or wauk mill at the north end of the town on the Noddle burn. So far as can be ascertained the latter had been a "burn" mill (i.e. it was operated by the flow of the water without any reserve supplies being kept in ponds) and the mills on the Gogo obtained their supplies from two separate but convergent lades, each with its own reserve storage pond (see fig. 28), one of which occupied the site of what is now part of Millburn Gardens.

With twentieth century manufacturing reliant on power from electric or internal combustion engines, we often overlook just how very important water was as a source of energy until very recently. In the case of Largs the processes which were especially important for woollen cloth were the wauking (or fulling) mill, the carding mill and the dye mill, whilst for linen production it was the lint mill.

Wauking (or fulling) involved beating the newly woven woollen cloth in water, to clean it and to felt (or "mat") it. Before water power came into use, the material was literally walked over in water (see fig. 29), but mechanisation made the process much less labour-intensive.

Carding involved a large drum with smaller drums rotating against it; all of these would have short, densely packed combs fitted to their surfaces (originally teasels but latterly metal) disentangling and aligning fibres prior to spinning (in 19th century Scotland it was quite common for this process to be mechanised whilst spinning still continued by hand). The dye mill would have rollers to crush the dye material, and water would also drive paddles in the vats.

In the case of linen, the initial problem was to separate the basic linen thread from the coarse bark or outer covering of flax. As a first step, flax was soaked in retting ponds like those in the Brisbane Glen already referred to, which softened

Fig. 29. Laborious feet wauking (fulling) of woollen cloth.
From a drawing by Miss J Logan.

the outer covering. Before suitable machinery became available, the next step was to beat flax with hammers, and then to scrape off the bark manually — a long laborious task — but with the invention of the lint mill (an outline drawing of its working parts is contained in fig. 30) much of the manual labour was eliminated. This was done by putting the softened stalks through rollers "E", and then the broken stalks were held against a scutching roller at the top, where bark was separated from the spinnable material.

After water went through the mill it was returned to the lade which joined up with those from the other mills, before returning direct to the Gogo, being fed over an aqueduct to the distillery, or used to flush waste from open sewers that ran down the main streets of Largs.

Whilst the location of the dye mill and carding mill can be easily ascertained (see fig. 28), that of the lint mill is unknown.

When electricity was installed (c.1933) to power the last remaining (saw)mill waterpower ceased to be used.

The first mention of any mill in the area appears about 1630 but indications are that one was in operation before that time. A John Osborne was tenant of one from 1671 to 1699, and Robert Thomson occupied a lint mill in 1787 shortly after the mill was build at the request of "the heritors and farmers in Kilbride parish" and with financial assistance from the National Exchequer. He could not have stayed there long, as by 1790 very little flax was being grown in the parish although, admittedly, the crop still being grown on Cumbrae might well have been sent to Largs for processing before being returned to the island for spinning and weaving in the subsidised unit provided by Captain Crawford, master of the the Cumbrae Revenue Cutter, for the benefit of the wives of his crew members.

Perhaps rather surprisingly, at this relatively late date, the help given by the National Exchequer towards the construction of the mill was based on a provision contained in the Treaty of Union of 1707, under which assistance was to be given to certain specified industries in Scotland including linen production.

A further known period of occupancy of the lower mill was from 1834 to 1867 when the tenants were Whiteford and Morris who advertised themselves as Corn, Flour, and Barley Millers.

Another mill on the Gogo was built in 1840 to weave wool but had rapidly run into financial problems, and only three years later, after it had ceased trading, the building was bought by Charles Scott of Halkshill who donated the stones to be used in the construction of the Free Church, now St John's.

Not that milling was the only activity that went on in the area. A family of Beiths worked a farm from at least 1760, and some of the Hyndman family seem to have worked land in the neighbourhood from at least 1736. Later, members of this

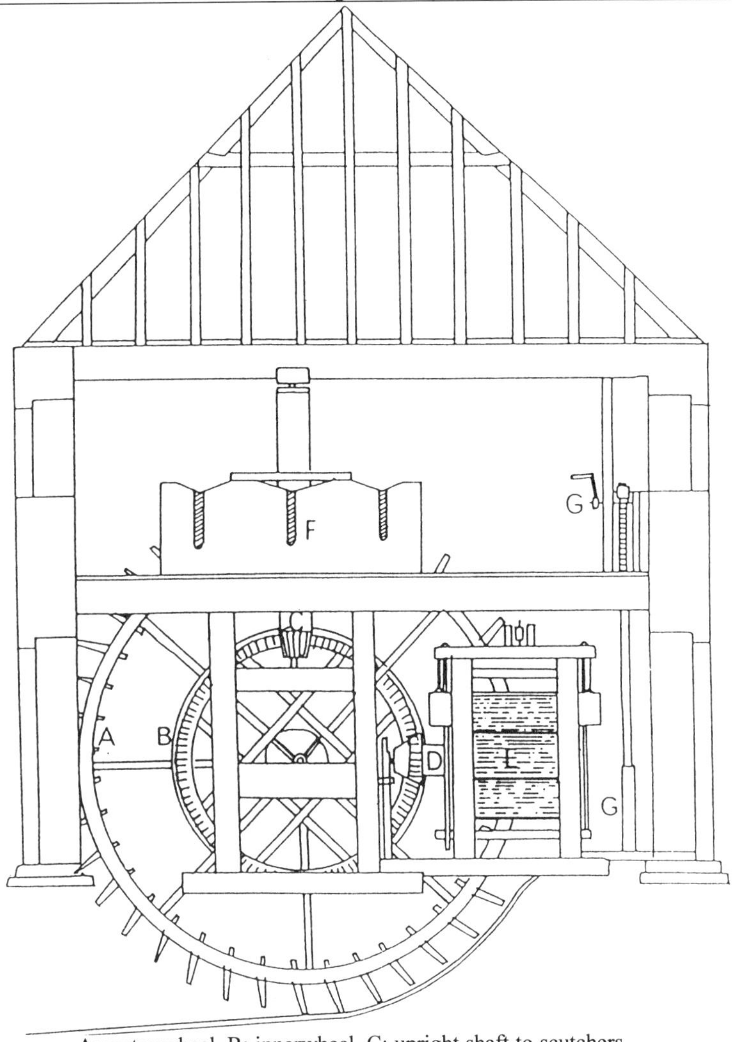

A: water wheel. B: innerwheel. C: upright shaft to scutchers.
D: lying shaft to rollers. E: breaking rollers.
F: scutching rollers.G: sluice control.

Fig. 30. Diagrammatic plan of scutching mill.

(Reproduced from "Waterpower in Scotland" by kind permission of Dr John Shaw.)

latter family took up feus in the town. (It will also be recalled Hyndman's Green now forms the open space outside the railway station.)

The first dwelling to occupy the south east corner site of the intersection of Gogoside Road and Irvine Road was known as Millburn House (see fig. 31), which was replaced in the mid-1930s by the Viking Cinema, which, in turn, became a bonded store in the 1970s. Demolished in 1983, a block of retirement flats known as Homemount now stands there.

About 200 yards further on towards Irvine we come to the site of a petrol sation on the north east side of the road, and we cannot help but wonder what made someone hide the small hoard of silver coins discovered near there sometime about 1840 (the Ordnance Survey notes are unable to give a precise date). As the actual coins seemed to vanish with the workmen, all that survives to tell of the incident is the name "Silver Rae" now given to the flatted development that has superseded the house which first occupied the site. A picture of how the house looked is shown in fig. 32.

Leaving the exploration of Douglas Park and the Neolithic tomb for another day, we cross Irvine Road and retrace our steps as far as Charles Street where we turn down towards the sea. A little way down we see on our left what was the former Charleston Hotel. The house on which this was based was built by Robert Lang and called "Blackdales". Bought by the court photographer John Fergus about 1876, it was his combined home and studio in which he had a gallery displaying photographs of the famous and not-so-famous. He later opened a second studio in Cannes, where he was wont to spend the "Riviera Season" each winter.

Although photography was still in its infancy, John Fergus not only successfully mastered the new technique of "wet collodion" introduced by Frederick Scott Archer in 1851 as a replacement for the earlier "daguerreotype" photography, but also built into his work the effect of his artistic talent. This combination ensured that his fame spread nation-wide. Probably his best known portrait is that of Gladstone, the Prime Minister. The severe unsmiling pose, elbows resting on the arms of a chair, and an unseen head restraint were all typical ploys used to overcome the problems encountered when a sitter had to stay absolutely still for the long exposure time then needed. Fergus died in 1908 as a result of a fall on a staircase.

At the seaward end of Charles Street, below us, if we look slightly to our right, we can see the Campbell Fountain which honours the memory of Dr John Campbell (1791-83), a local doctor who practised in the Gallowgate in Largs for over sixty years. Paid for by public subscription, the fountain's water was first turned on in 1878, but when, in 1880 a decision was taken to move it from its original site in

Fig. 31. Former Millburn House, Irvine Road, Largs.
(From collection of Largs and District Historical Society.)

Fig. 32. Original Silverae House, Irvine Road, Largs.
(From the collection of Largs and District Historical Society.)

Greenock Road opposite the Royal Hotel (now Morriss's), Mr Scott of Halkshill provided the necessary funds. To put it in the best position possible, the ground level had to be raised (the previous lower level had been used for parking fishing boats out of season).

If we then turn left we pass a block of modern flats known as Castle Bay Court. This was built in the 1960s on the site of what had been Broomfield House. From 1940-42 this was the HQ of No 3 Commando under the command of Lord Lovat. During this period the property suffered badly (it was used as a store for about twenty motor cycles and a ton of ammunition). Besides being used as a store it was also used for training in many unusual subjects, including how to get into locked buildings and safes where no key was available — the instructors, it is understood, were brought from prison for the purpose.

The Elderslie Hotel was initially built as two separate houses: Elderslie House in 1812 as the local UP manse, and Priory Lodge in 1829 for Henry Dunlop who had shipping interests. Bought by Mr J Wilson, a chartered accountant, in 1911 they were linked by a corridor with the intention of also adding baths to make them the "Largs Hydropathic". Unfortunately the outbreak of the First World War prevented this happening, and the economic climate in the early twenties did not favour such a project.

During World War II, these buildings were run by WRNS as a rest home for Fleet Air Arm pilots between spells of duty. It is also understood Lord Mountbatten was nursed there for a foot injury. Next to Broomfield House had stood a small tearoom which in World War II was turned into a private primary school.

Rev John Leach, minister of the local dissenting congregation, seems to have occupied his manse until 1851 when it was bought by Miss Speirs. She added the back premises and wings. Her family, who were mill owners in Elderslie, are thought to have claimed descent from the Scots hero, William Wallace. The heraldic insignia of this family can still be seen on the south facing wall above the dining room, and an examination of the roof will reveal the decorations in the form of chess pieces which were part of the original design.

After the brothers Dunlop the next occupiers of Priory Lodge were lawyers: Dr James Graham of Messrs J A & J Graham, Glasgow, and then Mr John Gill SSC, Chairman of Arizona Copper Co who bought it in 1905. He died in 1911.

At one time this corner had been the stage for a very interesting scenario. The brothers Dunlop who had built Priory Lodge, and some of their neighbours, were not content with just their open outlook. They also wanted more privacy, so they erected pillars (see fig. 48) to restrict access by the general public. This annoyed many locals, who enlisted the support of Sir Thomas Brisbane for the demolition of these obstructions. On the date set for this to be done, a large crowd assembled

Fig. 33. Original Curling Hall.
(From the Largs and District Historical Society Collection.)

Fig. 34. Original Barra House later to form part of Marine & Curlinghall Hotel.
(From the Largs and District Historical Society Collection.)

to watch Sir Thomas strike the first blow. The task completed, a cheering crowd removed the horses from Sir Thomas's carriage, put him into it, and pulled him and his carriage along the newly-opened road.

Prior to the "New Town" development, the area literally consisted of fields of broom, so it is not surprising the whole area was known as "Broomfields" and Broomfield Crescent was the name given to the front street (although this was first known as Brisbane Place). In the 1980s a new housing development was built on the site of the former Marine and Curlinghall Hotel, which, like the Elderslie, was originally two separate buildings. One was "Curling Hall", designed by David Hamilton, and built in 1812 for John Cairnie, a curling enthusiast who was to become first President of the Royal Caledonian Curling Club. So enthusiastic was he that a curling pond designed by himself was incorporated in the grounds of his house. Lined with clay, so that it froze over before other ponds, this is thought to have been the first ever manmade curling pond. In winter, when the pond was ready for playing he had a special flag flown to let everyone know.

During the building of Curling Hall, some Bronze Age cists were discovered, but the relative stones were used as building materials.

Two Victorian wings were added by its next owner, Mr John Clark of Anchor Thread Mills in Paisley, who later was to donate the Clark Memorial Church to the community.

The other part of the hotel, "Barra House", had been used as a rest home for wounded service men during World War I, Afterwards it became the "Marine Hotel", and when linked to Curling Hall in 1957 the accommodation available included 90 bedrooms, 350 dining places, and room for 600 dancers. How this looked at the various stages of its life can be seen in figs 33 (Curling Hall), 34 (Barra House), and 35 (Marine and Curlinghall).

Fortunately, the wonderful wooden panelling of the entrance hall was not destroyed when the building was demolished in 1982, but was sold separately and removed.

A little way along Broomfields is Littleraith — also thought to have been designed by David Hamilton. Named Broomfields Cottage when built by the Stevenson family, its one-storey Pavilion style with central bowed-projection makes it one of the most attractive villas in the town. At one time this was occupied by Andrew Montgomery, who besides being Provost, was also a partner in a local outfitters, Montgomery Clark.

The first house to appear at the corner of May Street was Crescent Lodge, now known as the South Bay Hotel. Previously it has been variously called the Sherwood Hotel and Picketlaw Hotel. The present structure is but little changed from the original.

Fig. 35. The Marine and Curlinghall Hotel, incorporating Barra House and Curlin Hall. (From the Largs and District Historical Society Collection.)

In the past, May Street has presented two ancient points of interest; a man and a horse buried together (as the horse bit has been identified as being Iron Age it seems unlikely it was a remnant of the Battle of Largs), and a number of Bronze Age burial cists, some of the remains of which can be seen in the old churchyard behind Manse Court.

Going on to the promenade we turn left, proceeding southwards. In so doing we find ourselves on a concreted pathway originally constructed with funds provided by a body of regular visitors known as the Largs Visitors' Club. Their aim was to create work for the unemployed, whilst at the same time improving amenities for visitors.

Towards the end of this "promenade", the road runs into the flatted development known as Bowen Craig, beside which is Warren Park Nursing Home. The first house on this site was constructed in 1866 for the Lang family, and was bought for £1,000 in 1905 by Mr Philippi, a director of J & P Coats. It was used as a convalescent home for the wounded in World War I, but subsequently reverted to being a private house. Then in 1924 the owner, Mr J S Paul, donated it to the British Red Cross Society who made it over to the East Park Home for Infirm Children. Its use as such continued until the 1980s. The main building of the Children's Home now survives as a Nursing Home.

Soon we enter open parkland which gives us a wonderful view of the area where at least some of the fighting must have taken place at the Battle of Largs in 1263. From this vantage point the difficulties that Vikings encountered in trying to land men and equipment from longships in the face both of the Scottish army and an equinoctial gale are only too clear.

Looking over to Meikle (or Great) Cumbrae we can see the steading of a farm on the slope facing towards us. Known as Portrye (thought to be derived from the Gaelic "Port an Righ" or "King's Port"), tradition has it that King Haakon watched at least part of the battle from there. Not far from the farm is a field still known by its Norse name of "Keil Fauld", or field of the chapel, where, again by tradition, Haakon said Mass at a small chapel before the battle.

In front of us is "The Pencil" monument, erected in 1912 to commemorate the Battle. Said to have been modelled on round towers of Brechin and Abernethy, it stands about seventy feet high and is a very interesting focal point in the long view down the Firth which is shown in fig. 36. This picture also includes the now demolished Rockland, of which we shall hear more below.

Beyond "The Pencil" lies Largs Marina which berths many of the yachts formerly anchored in Largs Bay. Moving them may have made the bay less scenic from the viewpoint of the visitor, but the yacht owners can sleep more soundly on stormy nights in the knowledge that their "treasures" are safe.

Fig. 36. Former Rockland, Irvine Road, Largs, with view to Pencil Monument and Portrye Farm on Cumbrae. (From the Largs and District Historical Society Collection.)

To return to our starting point at the pier we now have a choice of two routes. We can either retrace our steps, or we can go back by the main Irvine Road to Largs. If we use the latter route to reach the Irvine Road, we must cross the railway either by the road bridge, or we can go under it by the pedestrian subway locally known as "Tinker's Bridge". Whichever we choose, when we arrive at the main road we turn left and proceed uphill towards the town.

The road is a very busy one, but there are one or two features worthy of note. First of all there is Largs Golf Club on the east side of the road. Formed in 1891 the club first played over a nine hole course on what is now part of Routenburn Golf Club. The club moved to its present location in what were the policies of Kelburn Castle in 1893, still as a nine hole course, but it was upgraded to the present 18 hole course in 1953.

On our left is a modern housing development in the grounds of the former "Rockland" referred to above. This was a substantial Victorian villa and when built for the Donaldson family of shipping fame it even had its own cinema - a very up-market feature for the time. Like many such buildings it later became an hotel (Redcourt Hotel), and, in common with many similar buildings, was "called up" for National Service in World War II when it served as the administrative head-quarters for the Fleet Air Arm. During this period it was known as "HMS Fara-way" (someone must have had their tongue in their cheek when that name was chosen). In 1958 it became "Red Cross House". This was a small factory unit with living accommodation attached which was specially adapted for physically handi-capped adults. It closed in 1985, and was demolished in 1994.

A little further on, the road which goes off on our right leads up the Haylie Brae. This is known locally as the old "Hourat Road" to Dalry which was initially the main road — that which now leads straight to Kilbirnie was defined as a branch road — and takes us past the cemetery to the viewpoint at the top of the hill. Without a footpath, as the road is narrow and very busy, it is not recom-mended that this be approached on foot. A little up the hill stands the former toll house which was used to collect dues when the road was run by a Turnpike Trust.

Going back towards the town, Haylie House is on our right. The original house was demolished by Richard Brown, a colliery owner who in 1885 replaced it sub-stantially in the form we now know. He sold the property to James Stevenson who was later both to gift the Stevenson Institute to the town and also to transfer to it, for a very nominal consideration, the ownership of Haylie House itself.

Until 1991, when a serious fire put the future status of the building in some doubt, Haylie House had served as an Old Folks' Home for many years. However, the completely refurbished premises were reopened in 1994 in the same capacity.

Nearer the town, also on our right, is the entrance to Douglas Park donated for

Fig. 37. Standing out amongst the trees, now largely felled, the original Burnmouth, Greenock Road, Largs, demolished to provide site of St Mary's R C Church.
(From Collection of Largs and District Historical Society.)

public use by Mr C J Douglas of Haylie. The entrance to this park also gives access to the Neolithic tomb on the hill behind. From here we return to the pier before setting out to explore what was to have been Brisbane New Town.

Designed with the intention that it would be composed of rather smaller houses than those which had been built in Gogo New Town, its starting date seems to have been delayed by legal problems, and it was 1824 before these appear to have been resolved. The anticipated demand for houses had not materialised, so whilst the intention had been to provide two blocks of terraced houses and a large number of smaller villas, with ornamental gardens between them and the Greenock Road, the only properties to be built more or less as originally planned, are Aubery Crescent and Vanduara, with ornamental gardens on the sea side only. The full effect of this change of plan will become apparent later, but if, for the moment, we proceed up Greenock Road from its junction with Nelson Street, we first of all pass Nardini's cafe, which we have already discussed. The next interesting building along the North Esplanade is Brisbane House Hotel, which began life as a terrace of four houses known as Cochrane's Buildings, which were later joined up to form St Helen's Hotel.

Next we come to Brooksby at 18 Greenock Road. This was designed for Matthew Perston as a holiday home by David Hamilton, and was built about 1843. Stones for the building came from a quarry near Girvan, Ayrshire, and were transported to Largs by sea. One of the vessels sank during a storm and, if some of the building (particularly the stable block) is examined carefully, the salvaged stones can be identified by their slight discoloration. In 1897 it was gifted by the then owner Mr Cooper to Glasgow's Victoria Infirmary, who opened it as the Victoria Home for Convalescents. Now it is under the management of the Ayrshire and Arran Trust Community Health Care NHS Trust.

Next to Brooksby is Moorburn. What we now see is not the first house to occupy the site. The first Moorburn was built by Dr Hugh Morris, a native of Largs who had returned home from the West Indies. When he died in 1813 it was taken over by his nephew Captain (later Major) Robert Morris. His occupancy of the house was followed by that of Robert Aitken in 1870, a retired Glasgow stockbroker, who was later to become the first provost of Largs (1876). He demolished the first house and built what we see today. In 1936 it became the offices of the Town Council, and is now the local office of Cunninghame District Council.

When the original house was being built it is understood some stone Bronze Age burial cists were discovered in the grounds, but no further details are available.

The Roman Catholic Church, St Mary Star of the Sea, was constructed in the grounds of the former "Burnmouth" (see fig. 37) which the congregation acquired

Fig. 38. Former Mansfield House, Largs, demolished to provide site of Barrfields Pavilion, now incorporated in the Vikingar!
(From Collection of Largs and District Historical Society.)

Fig. 39. Former St. Columba manse, Greenock Road, Largs, being demolished in c1936 to allow speculative housing development.
(From Collection of Largs and District Historical Society.)

in the 1950s for about £5,000. The church opened for worship on 24th June 1962, but unfortunately almost immediately part was very badly damaged by fire and some services had to be held in The Moorings while repair work was carried out.

The large granite statue fronting the building is the work of Hew Lorimer, and the light colour of the stone contrasts well with the background of Westmorland slate of the facade.

We come now to a number of modern bungalows built by a property developer after 1956. These stand on land shown in the 1805 map as "Toun Land" and as such was part of the town's common grazing before becoming glebe land attached to the manse. Past these bungalows we come to the new "Vikingar!", formerly Barrfields Pavilion, with its leisure amenities. This pavilion, the Springfield Hotel next door, and the adjacent modern houses stand on the site of a former Victorian villa named Mansfield. A picture of the house as it was appears in fig. 38, and a photograph of the manse demolished in the 1930s appears in fig. 39.

The 1805 map also describes some of the lands here as South Kirklands and, whilst the import of this description is not wholly clear, they, and North Kirklands which lie to the north of the Noddle burn, probably had some connection with the lands granted to the Brisbanes by John Hamilton, Archbishop of St Andrews as commendator at Paisley Abbey in 1557.

Mansfield was once the home of Dr Hugh Lang who had also made his fortune in the West Indies, and who was one of the first to order a purpose-built yacht from Fifes of Fairlie. The house and land, bought by Mr Robert Barr in 1925, were donated by him to the Town Council along with £1,000 towards the erection of the pavilion which has been substantially extended in 1995. Formally opened by his widow in 1930, the name Mansfield was changed to Barrfields.

Born on Constablewood Farm where his father was a tenant, Robert Barr was an outstanding example of a local boy made good. He made at least two fortunes, one in whisky and another in shipping. Not only was he generous to Largs, he gifted Kirkton House and Glen to West Kilbride, where he also met the cost of constructing two bowling greens.

As we have seen, during World War II the pavilion became a maintenance base for seaplanes. Initially these were Sunderlands and Catalinas, with a few Walrus and Kingfisher aircraft that also came in from time to time. One of the Catalinas sank in a position not far from the Cumbrae ferry terminal, and, because of the large number of fish that now populate them, the remains are a popular objective for scuba divers.

Not that this aircraft was the only local casualty. On another day a Sunderland pilot misjudged the water level (there was a low fog at the time) and ditched his aircraft, which was recovered and repaired later. Probably his greatest

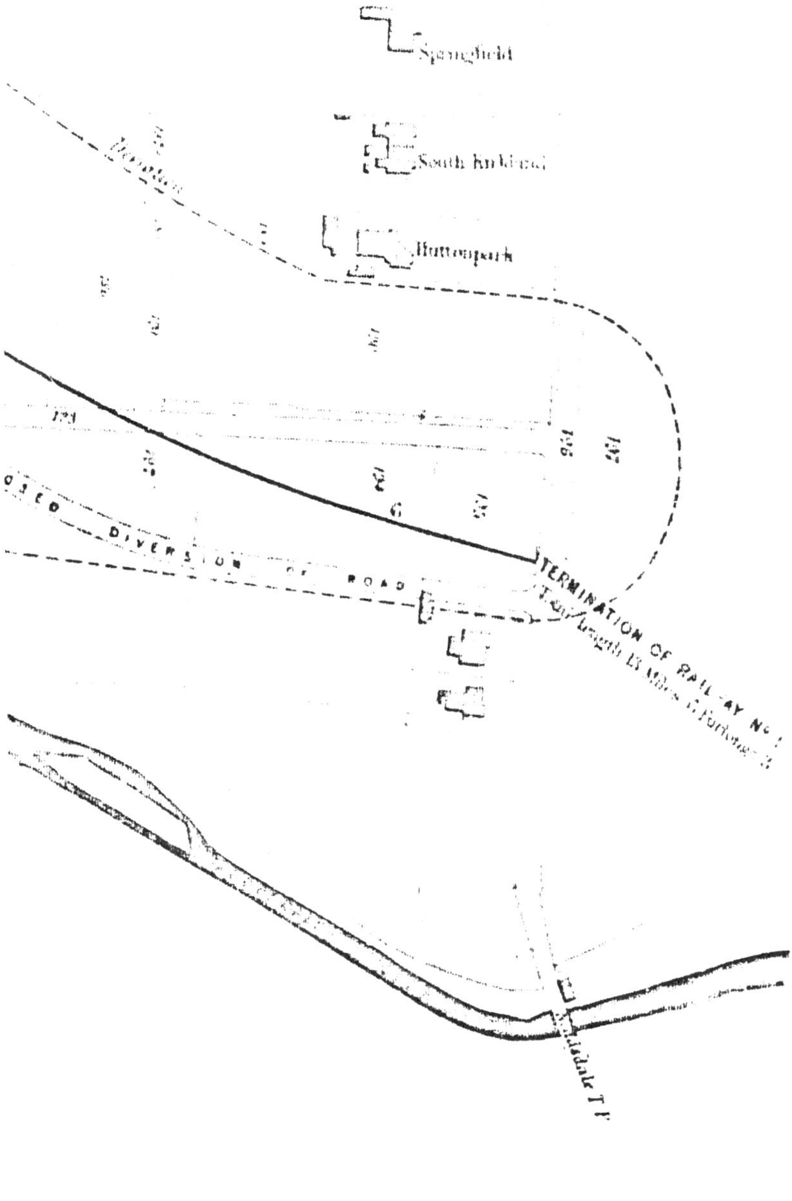

Fig. 40. Proposed area for siting of Largs terminal of railway from Dalry.

(Reproduced by permission of Keeper of Records of Scotland, from RHP 34877/1.)

embarrassment however, was to have his crew and himself rescued by two WRNS, out in one of Halliday's rowing boats!

By 1944 more and more aircraft were using the facilities at Barrfields, including aircraft known as Cornados (the seaplane version of the Liberator bomber), and Martin Mariners. As a result Largs became something like an international airport with a daily service to and from Montreal, (with one direct leg, but returning via Iceland), and a weekly service to Nigeria.

When not in the air the aircraft were moored in Balloch Bay off Cumbrae, and on one count the numbers lying there were 18 Catalinas, 2 Cornados and 2 Martin Mariners.

Past Barrfields we can turn right and go up Brisbane Street and then via Brisbane Road and Burnside Road to Inverclyde Sports Centre. Originally (1775) known as Burnside farm, the present main building is basically what was erected as a home for Mr R S Scott about 1877, before becoming the Hills Hotel in the 1920s. It was used during World War II as the HQ of the First Army, and then became the home of Lord Inverclyde. He died before the Centre was opened by the Queen in 1957.

If, from the Queens Hotel, we do not go to the Sports Training Centre, but continue north along the Greenock Road, we shall pass through the area that was to have been the terminal of the railway line from Dalry (see fig 40), and then come to all that was built of the original grandiose "Brisbane New Town" plan, namely a large villa, Vanduara, now divided into flats, and a crescent of terraced houses (Aubery Crescent).

The villa was originally named "Fon-na-Mara", a name which was changed to "Vanduara" by Mr James Clark, who resided there before he purchased Curling Hall. It was also the name he had given to one of his yachts based on a name he was told the Romans had given to what is now Paisley.

At the start of World War II Vanduara, still an hotel run by Mr William Derby, was requisitioned for war service. In a somewhat unusual move Mr Derby was asked to stay on and cater for the naval unit which occupied it. This he agreed to do, and was immediately appointed to the rank of chief petty officer in the Navy. It is said that it was here that the planning conference for the D Day landings was held.

The original plan for what was to become Aubery Crescent was amended to allow for the site of St Columba's Episcopal Church and its manse. In the 1980s the manse was sold as a private house, and modern flats were constructed in what had been the manse garden.

Although the church was constructed in 1877, the main part of the housing development does not seem to have proceeded until after 1884. Just how this was

Fig. 41. Former Woodbank, Greenock Road, Largs, now replaced by flatted development.
(From the Largs and District Historical Society Collection.)

Fig. 42. Former Kirklands/Rosebank, Greenock Road, Largs.now replaced by speculative housing development.
(From The Largs and District Historical Society Collection.)

financed is not clear, but there is some indication of a possible involvement by Robert Wallace, a developer who had plans for the "Marine Village" of Skelmorlie.

Behind Aubery Crescent is Aubery Park, through which Noddsdale Water flows. As can be seen from fig. 1, in 1805, before being feued out for Brisbane New Town, this area was let out to the townspeople in acre plots. Some of these would be weavers from the town who wished to augment their food supply. It should perhaps be explained that some Largs weavers rented small plots of land, fertilised them with material taken from the dungheaps at their own back doors, planted out their own crops there, and then harvested the produce. The dungheaps resulted from their keeping pigs and cows in the yards behind their houses.

In later times the park was used as a local cricket field.

When we come out of the park on to Greenock Road we find ourselves at the bridge over the Noddle Burn. This was first constructed in 1736, widened by the Turnpike Road Commissioners in 1824 so that it could be used by coaches, and further widened on a number of occasions since. Besides collecting dues from travellers and dispensing appropriate refreshments, the toll house (also constructed in 1824) served another important function, as, before they had their own church, Roman Catholics regularly worshipped there. Collection of tolls, both here and at Haylie, ceased in 1880.

Just over the bridge, but on the other side of the road, stands what was the entrance lodge of Netherhall. This and the main house (now part of a speculative development) were built in 1876 for Lord Kelvin's retirement. An imposing example of Scottish Baronial architecture, the red sandstone building, set amidst attractively landscaped grounds, did not meet with universal approval. The story is told of one lady attending a reception there, who had not hesitated to express her feelings to a gentleman standing nearby. Nor did she confine herself to conveying these feelings of disapproval, she also expanded on the treatment she felt should be meted out to the architect responsible for the design. Unfortunately she was met with the somewhat embarrassing response that he was just that architect!

Although imposing, the house was also functional; it was said to have been the first house in Scotland to be equipped with electric light; it also had a central heating system.

After Lord Kelvin's death in 1907, the house, with stables, a wash-house and a joiner's yard, became first an hotel, and later a Christian Guest House/Conference Centre. Sold to property developers in 1987, the house has been turned into flats, and modern houses have been erected in the grounds. As with so many similar properties in Largs, in World War II, Netherhall was used for military purposes and housed a unit of WRNS.

Fig. 43. Former Landour, Greenock Road, Largs. now replaced by a speculative housing development. (From the Largs and District Historical Society Collection.)(By courtesy of Miss F Ferguson.)

The 1805 map (fig. 1) reveals that a "wauk mill" for treating woven wool had once stood on the Noddle Burn near here.

If we wish, at this point we can divert eastwards up Routenburn Road, locally nicknamed the "Red Road" and descriptive of the soil in the area. Other local names also apply to it: "Forgie Brae" refers to the lower slope, "The Regularity Road" to the climb up to the summit and the "back road to Greenock" to the whole road.

On our left is the golf course which although it is now the home of Routenburn Golf Club, is where Largs Golf Club started playing before it moved to its present site in 1893. After being opened as a nine hole course in 1913, it was remodelled in 1919 by James Baird a famous professional golfer. The imposing clubhouse (originally "Netherpark") was bought for the club by the Town Council in 1930, and is still leased by the club from Cunninghame District Council.

Luckily, a proposal to build a railway line from Wemyss Bay to Largs did not materialise, as the adverse effect this would have had on the scenic beauty on this part of the town would have been disastrous.

Going north, once we pass Netherhall, we are in a road which in the early 1800s was lined by a number of very large villas, some of which, due to changing economic climates, have given way to flatted developments. Whilst in a few cases some information is available about individual houses, on the whole little is known of their backgrounds.

The somewhat irregular order of their erection is set our below. For this there seems no apparent reason, although the legal difficulties encountered may well have had some effect.

Const. Date	*Street Number*	*Comments*
1813	-	South Kirklands House (Queen's Hotel);
1816	170	Routenburn;
1834	96	Woodbank, and
	100	Rosebank; now both demolished and replaced by flats;
	124	Northfield, now flatted as part of an overall modern development in conjunction with Landour.
1845	112	Elmbank, now flatted; and
	118	Landour, now replaced by modern houses;
1848	52	Hutton Park and
	54	Springfield.
1850	106	Haus Saron (formerly Morven);
1873	136	Underbank; now replaced by flats.
1885	148	Danefield, now flatted.

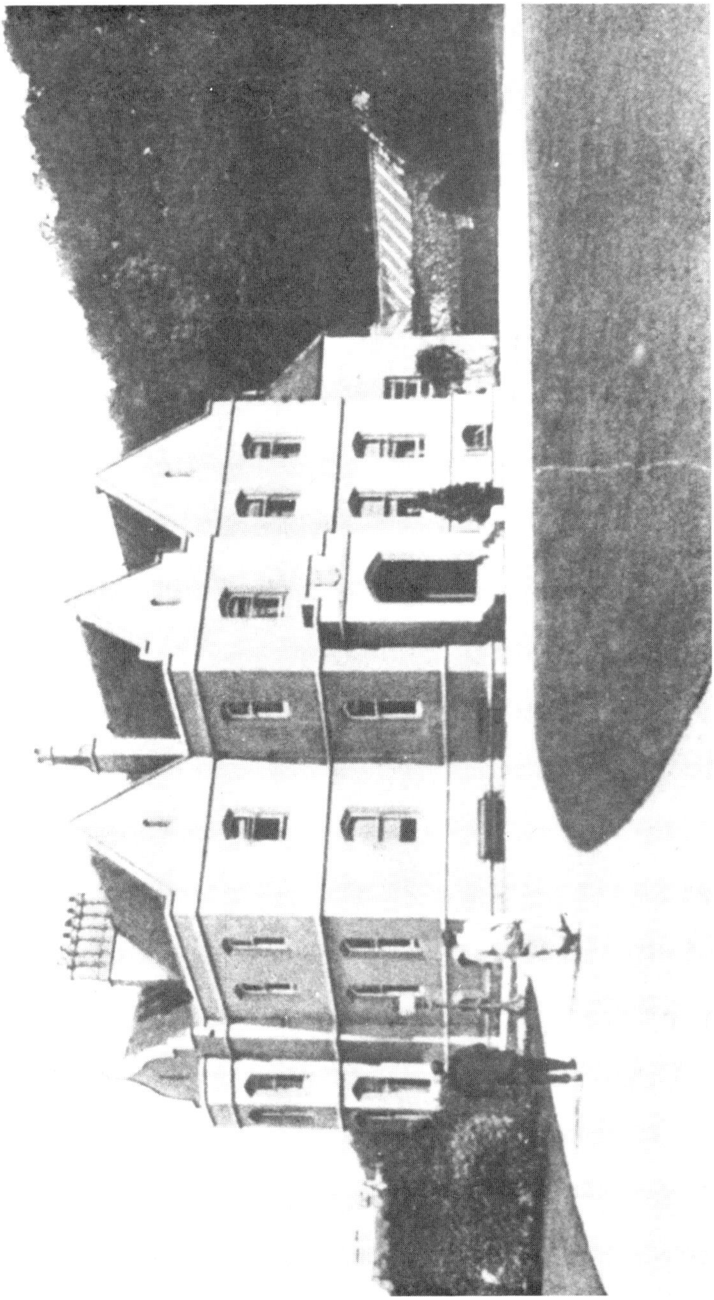

Fig. 44. Former Underbank (Hollywood), Greenock Road, Largs, now replaced by blocks of flatted development. (From the Largs and District Historical Society Collection. By courtesy of Miss F Ferguson.)

The following details of occupants of some of these properties may be of interest:

Street Number

52 Hutton Park was built for Thomas Hutton Inglis and is now a retirement home.

54 The Springfield Hotel was occupied as a residence as far back as 1848, and became an hotel sometime before 1957.

96 Woodbank (see fig. 41) was originally feued to Dr Thomas Brisbane in 1834. Subsequent occupants included Dr William Hunter (1871), and Ebenezer Ramsay (1884), before passing to the Simpson family in 1929. They occupied it until 1978 when it was demolished to make way for flats.
The Simpson family, printers and stationers in the town, were a well known local family. Founders of the Largs and Millport Weekly News (the "Wee Paper"), they were the first to demonstrate and sell that contraption known as "wireless" in the town.
Alexander Simpson travelled on the first train to run from Largs Station in 1885, and became the second Freeman of Largs in 1963. (The first such honour was bestowed on King Haakon of Norway in 1944.)

96 The Willowbank Hotel was built in the grounds of the former Woodbank.

100 Kirklands, originally Rosebank (see fig. 42) was built on land feued to Wilhemina Richardson in 1853. Other occupants included George B Hoggan (1900), W Kerr (1860), and Mrs Holms (1892). Then it seems to have become an hotel run by various people including families by the name of Thornes, Madden, and Kerr.
It was demolished in 1974 and replaced by flats.

106 Morven was built for a Colonel Morris and was renamed Haus Saron.

112 Elmbank was built for Hugh Lang Kerr in 1845 and converted to flats in 1964. One of the early occupants of the property was Provost Eckford. The various gifts he and his family bestowed on the town were munificent indeed.

118 Landour (see fig. 43) was built in 1845 for Dr John Buchanan, from whom it passed to Thos McCunn in 1884, and then in 1894 to Wm McCunn who sold it to the Marist Brothers in 1920. From then, until 1987, St Columba's College as it was known, became a Primary Boarding School for boys, mainly, but not wholly, destined for St Joseph's in Dumfries.
The playing field on the opposite side of the road had become permanently unuseable after a torrential rainstorm in 1970, so it was sold to a property

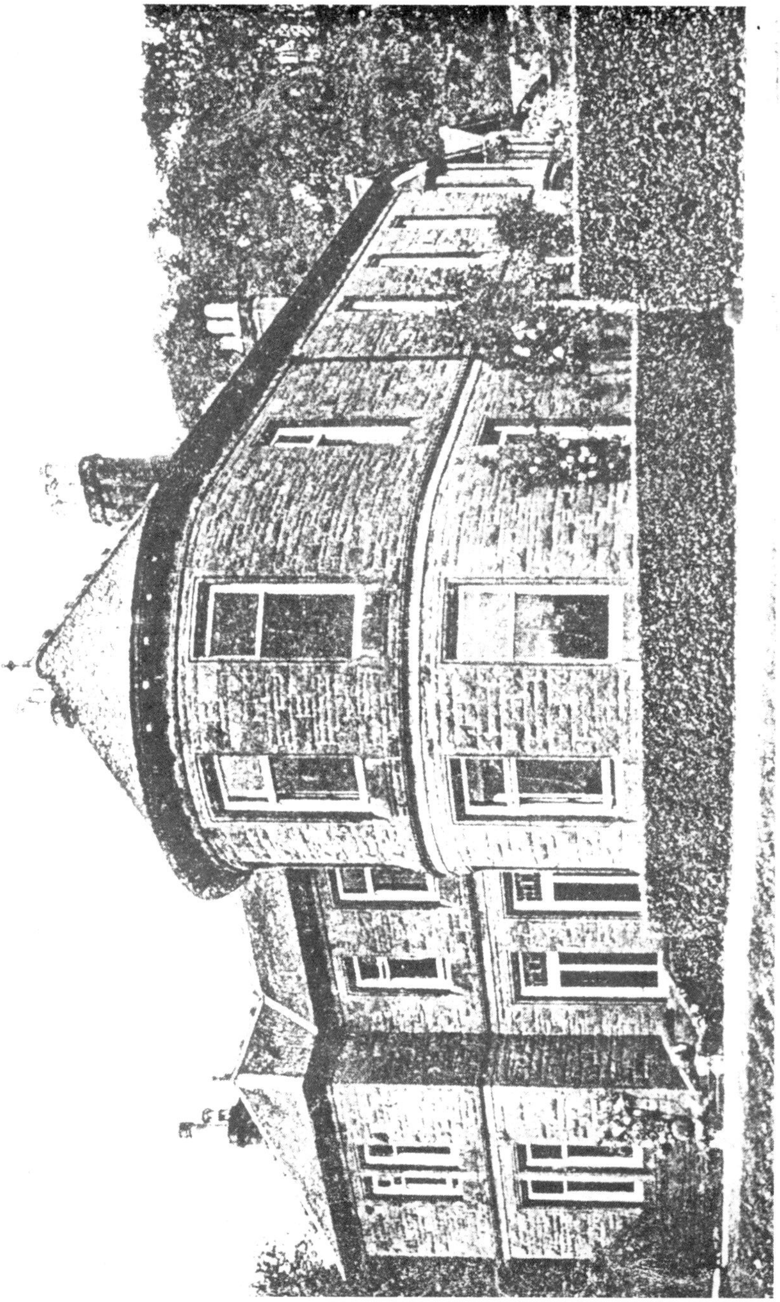

Fig. 45. Former Holmwood, Greenock Road, Largs, now replaced by speculative housing development. (From the Largs and District Historical Society Collection.)

developer. The proceeds went towards the purchase of Northfield (see below). Both properties were sold to a property developer in 1985 and Landour was demolished in 1991.

124 Northfield was constructed in 1834/35 in the style of David and James Hamilton. It was occupied by a family of Robertsons until it was sold in 1867 to the Rev Charles Watson. He lived there with his wife and family until 1908, when the house was sold to Mr John Henderson, a retired silk merchant. His daughter Mrs Ferguson inherited the property and lived there until 1971, when it was sold to the Marist Brothers who incorporated it into St Columba's College (see Landour above). Along with Landour, it was sold to a property developer in 1985.

136 Underbank (Hollywood) (see fig. 44) was built for the Holms Kerr family who occupied it from 1873 to 1894. Thereafter it was occupied by a succession of families until it was extended to become the Hollywood Hotel in 1936.

During the Second World War it became the HQ of Combined Operations as HMS Warren (named by someone with a sense of humour?).

The story goes that the swimming pool was covered over to form the conference room where, "Operation Rattle" decided that the opening of the Second Front would take place in Normandy.

After the cessation of hostilities it became a convalescent home for the SCWS. This closed in 1982 and the site is now occupied by two sets of flats known as Underbank and Hollywood.

148 Danefield was erected about 1885 in the Scots Baronial style.

The first owner was Miss Jessie Graham Crum, younger sister of the first Lady Kelvin of Netherhall, and sister of the second wife of the Rev Charles Watson of Northfield.

Sold in 1914 to Mr Charles Cockburn, Manufacturing Chemist in Glasgow, his only daughter Mrs Dorothy Kelly, who had married the son of the Lord Provost of Glasgow, inherited the property.

After World War II she sold some of the grounds to property developers, and in the 1970s divided the house into flats.

164 Holmwood. This property was built in 1891 for Mr H J McCall, and became a holiday home for the staff of Collins (publishers) in 1947 (see fig. 45). It was demolished in 1965. At the sea side of the garden, there are the remains of a prehistoric fish trap.

170 Routenburn. Built in 1816 for Dr Lang, it also became a home for one of the Scotts of the Greenock shipbuilding family, who occupied it until 1892 when it became "a preparatory school for young gentlemen". Requisitioned

Fig. 46. Former Bonnyblink Tearoom at top of Haylie Brae, Largs.
(Reproduced by kind permission of Nicolson Maps, Largs.)

in World War I as a convalescent home for wounded soldiers, it again became an educational institution in 1921 as a preparatory school for Loretto Public School, in Musselburgh, near Edinburgh. In 1928 it was known as Clyde College, providing education up to university level. This closed in 1961.
The building was vandalised and then demolished.

The changes in the structure of society after World Wars I & II have meant that the "big houses" as such had to go. Whilst accepting this as a fact of life, it is still sad to recall the appearance of those grand houses that have fallen to the bulldozer. The greatest loss of all was of course the Marine and Curlinghall Hotel, but another smaller building was also sadly missed, if for a rather different reason. This was the Bonnyblink Tearoom of immediate pre World War II vintage (fig 46), and its marvellous vista of the Clyde which made it such a favourite spot for the teenage "courting" of a different era. The viewpoint which it replaces just does not have the same ambience!

* * *

In the preceding pages the reader has been asked to absorb a great deal of detailed information, and in many instances has been expected to use his (or her) imagination, so, in order to add to the understanding of the changes which have taken place on the seafront over the last century or so, two additional illustrations are provided in figs. 47 and 48. The first of these reproduces the panoramic view of the buildings between Nelson Street and Castle Brae to be affected by the proposed new railway station at the pier (although for some reason St Columba's Church is omitted). Whilst interesting for many reasons, attention is specially drawn to McQuiston's boat yard at the south end, the details of the frontage of Columba Hall, and also to the absence of both Sandringham and the Clark Memorial Church.

The second of the illustrations shows the shore line in 1845 before the construction of the various walkways we have today, and shows the small natural harbour which was then available on the south side of the Gogo. It also shows the prison and the pillars demolished as described on page 65 — both circled.

* * *

Perhaps before we go away to ponder all we have read and seen, we should go down to the shore near Holmwood, and look at the nearby remains of the Neolithic fish trap which can still be seen (if only just) on the shore opposite Haus Saron.

If this does not help us to put everything into perspective, perhaps a walk along the "Red Road", with all the beautiful views that can be seen from there, will be more successful. At the same time we might even return to our first thoughts, the

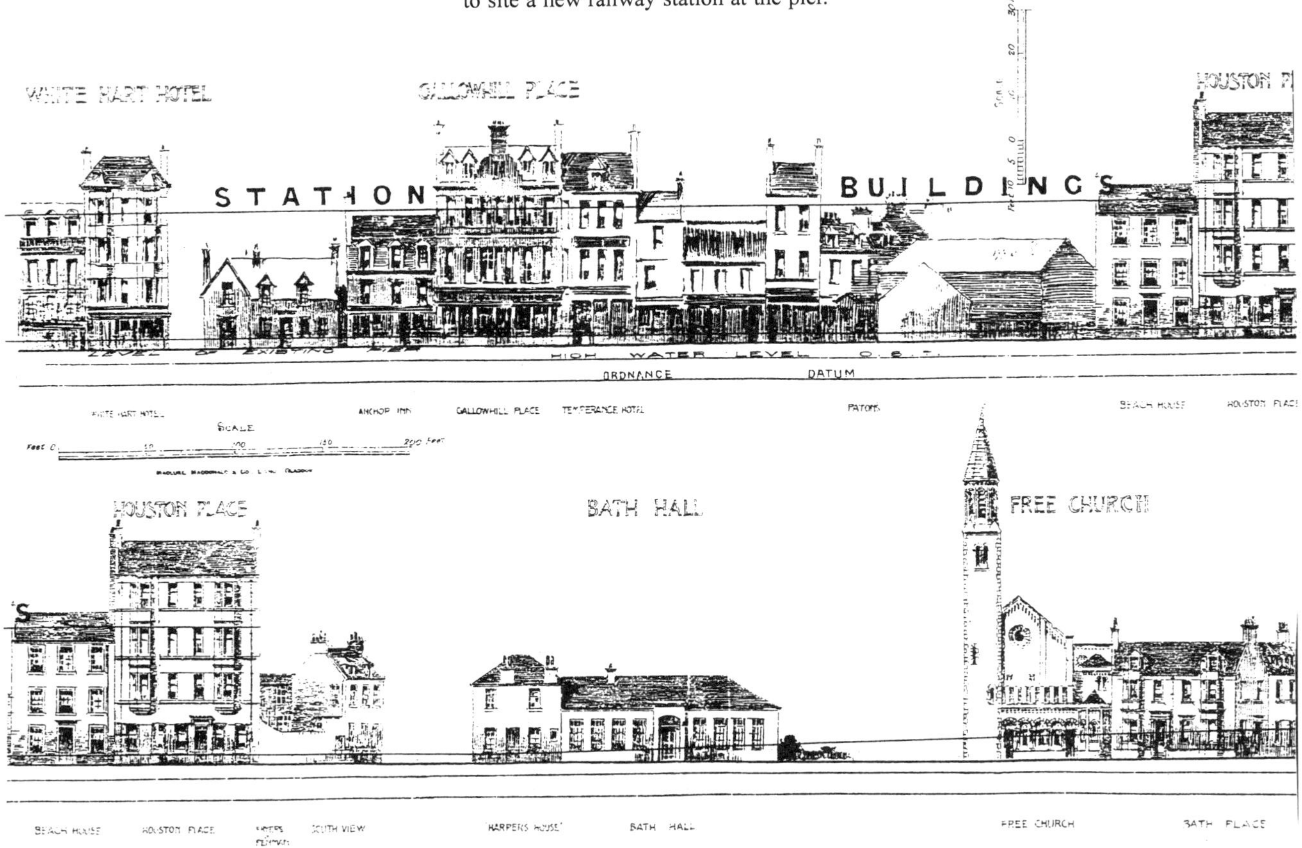

Fig. 47 Drawing of frontages of buildings facing the seafront at Largs c.1890 from a survey prepared for use in connection with a proposal to site a new railway station at the pier.

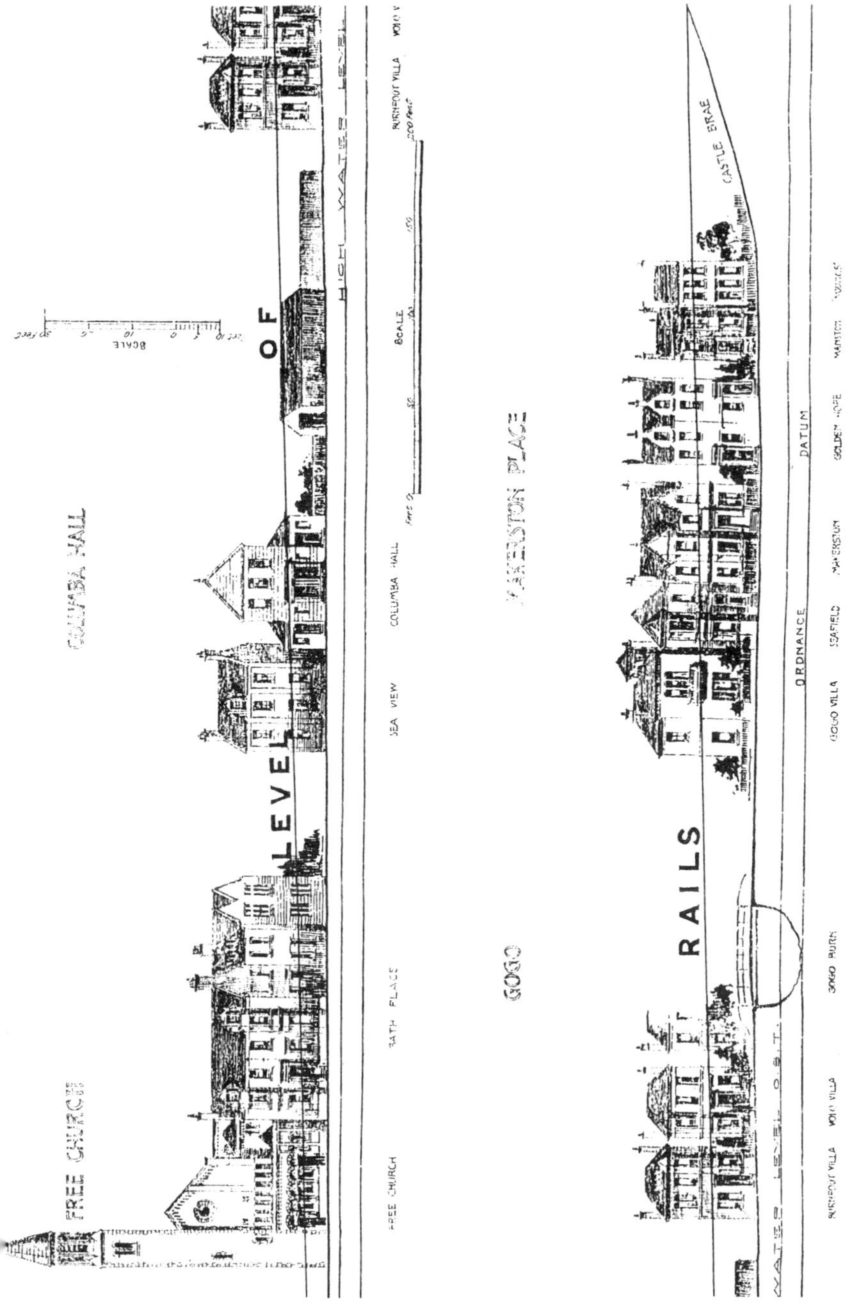

(Reproduced by kind permission of Mr W Topping, Largs.)

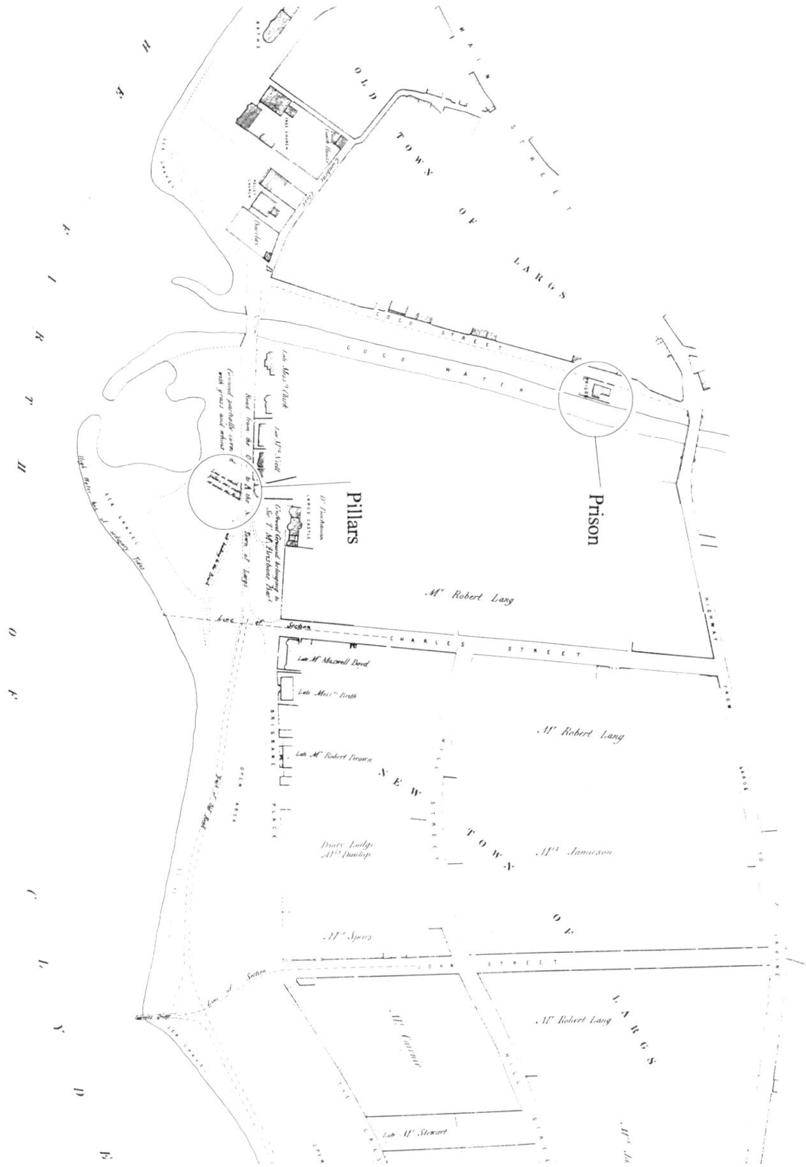

Fig. 48 The shore line at the mouth of the Gogo in 1845, before the construction of the various walkways in the early twentieth century, which resulted in the small natural harbour on the south shore being infilled.
(Reproduced by kind permission of Mr W. Topping, Largs)

derivation of local names. Killingcraig (or Billingcraig as it is described in the burghal charter) is probably reasonably easy to imagine as being a corruption of the Gaelic for either the cell on the hill, or the ferm toun on the hill, and Altburn (one of the ferm touns on the 1805 plan) is probably the combination of the Scots and Gaelic names for the same thing - a stream.

Some other thoughts are as follows:-

Dochra probably contains the Gaelic 'dubh', black and 'croabh' tree;

Gogo and Greeto probably originally had endings in -ach giving Gogach which would mean the place of nodding or cooing (as of pigeons);

Hangandsheuche in Scots, a hanging precipice;

Harplaw - probably 'harp hill';

Killburn (or Kilburn) - the first element is probably Gaelic 'Coille' wood;

Rylies (or Raillies) - rye lees -lea land where rye was grown;

Tourgill - Gaelic torr 'hill' and Scots/Norse 'gill' ravine;

Whittlieburn - could be from 'white lea', with burn the Scots word for stream.

ACKNOWLEDGEMENTS

Many people have contributed towards the completion of my manuscript, but I must especially thank Mr Nigel Tranter for his help and encouragement, without which I would have given up at a very early stage.

Others have given freely of their time and knowledge: Mrs Evie Corkill has typed many, many discs for me and has also done a very great deal of proofreading; Miss Sarah Goldie has helped enormously in the selection of illustrations and with proofreading; Mr John Chalmers has very generously allowed me to draw on his massive researches into buildings in Largs; Miss Fionna Ferguson, besides providing photographs for illustrations, has, along with Mrs Sheila Clinton, made available results of researches into the census records; Mrs Kay McCreadie has spent a considerable amount of time combing the archives of the Largs and District Historical Society for suitable photographs; Mr Stewart Clinton and Mr Frank Alexander have guided me on railway matters, Miss Valerie Bickers has similarly helped me on walks; Mr Malcolm Nicolson has generously adapted his Largs street plan to incorporate the various stages of the town's development and allowed me to use it here, and the Largs Bookshop has helped with photocopying; Mr Douglas Easton has provided the results of his researches into the Brisbane and Irvine archives, and has also, along with Dr Owen Gurton, helped with words of encouragement and advice in so many ways, and Mr Bill Topping has given me the benefit of his extensive local knowledge.

The staff of the Largs branch of the library service of Cunninghame District Council and of the Carnegie Library in Ayr have shown great patience and initiative in finding what I wanted, often from less than lucid instructions.

As always the staff of the Scottish Record Office, of the Map Room of the National Library of Scotland, of the School of Scottish Studies of Edinburgh University, and of the Strathclyde Regional Archives have all given freely of their time and guidance.

The art work produced for me by Ms Jacqui Logan, Kilbirnie, is of the highest order. That on the outer cover of the book represents a provost in the official gown and chain of the town, looking back over the past. Apart from Charles I who granted the first burghal charter to Largs, all the other characters shown are fictitious.

I would ask everyone to accept my very sincere thanks.

Last, but certainly by no means least, I am very grateful indeed for the ever continuing huge support and encouragement of my wife, Betty.

J R D Campbell.

BIBLIOGRAPHY

The following details of material I have consulted may serve as a starting point for those wishing to explore the history of Largs in more depth. (To save space I have left out details of publishers of the various works noted.) These are, of course, in addition to all the invaluable files of the Largs and Millport Weekly News.

I General Background Information

1. **National Records** For the County of Ayr: Old Statistical Account 1791 - 1799; New Statistical Account (Original) - 1845; Third Statistical Account - 1951 (New Strawhorn Edition); Register of Sasines; Report on Parochial Education in Scotland 1825/26.

2. **Other Sources** Ancient Church Dedications in Scotland - J O Mackinlay; Ayrshire, Its History and Historic Families - William Robertson; Bute in Early Christian Times - Rev J K Howieson; Isle of Bute in Olden Time - Rev Jas K Hewison; County of Bute - Eaton Reid; History of Bute - Blain; Biographical Dictionary of Eminent Scotsmen - Rev Thomas Thomson; Caledonia, Vols. I, III, IV and VII- George Chalmers; Calendars of Scottish Saints - A P Forbes; Carte Monialium de Northberwic - Bannatyne Club 1847; Chambers Scottish Biographical Dictionary - Rosemary Goring, Editor; Cunninghame - Timothy Pont, as edited by John Shedden Dobie; Education in Largs - Mrs M Murray (in Largs Historical Society Collection); An Historic Atlas of Scotland c.600 - c. 1600, Edited by Peter McNeill and Ranald Nicholson; Some Family Papers of the Hunters of Hunterston; Kelso of Kelsoland - Col. W R Kelso, San Diego (in Largs Historical Society Collection); Making of Urban Scotland -I H Adams; Ragman Rolls 1291/96 -Bannatyne Club 1884; Scotland 1689 to the Present - W Ferguson; Scotland in Early Christian Times - Joseph Anderson; Scottish Trade with Ireland in the 18th Century - L E Cochran; Topographical Description of Cunninghame - Geo. Robertson (1820).

II Local Authorities

1. **Financial Records:** Largs Poll Tax Roll 1698; Window Tax Roll 1760, 1765, 1770, 1773, 1774 and 1782.
2. **Minutes etc.:-** Largs Parochial Board - 1859 - 60; Ayrshire Constabulary Committee 1841 - 1886; Turnpike Road Trustees 1807 -1846; Ayr County Council; Largs Town Council; Millport Town Council.

3. **Other Sources:-** Burghs of Ayrshire - George S Pryde; Coat of Arms and Commentary - Arms of the Baronial and Police Burghs of Scotland; Charters relating to the City of Glasgow - Marwick and Renwick; The River Clyde and the Clyde Burghs - Marwick; History of Irvine - John Strawhorn; Muniments of Burgh of Irvine; Scottish Burghs - George S Pryde; Scottish County Government in the Eighteenth and Nineteenth Centuries - Anne E Whetstone; Tacksmen and their Successors - E R Gregeen.

III Trading Activities

1. **Farming**

a) **National Records:** Ministry of Agriculture and Fisheries - Parish Returns and Summaries 1886 -1980.

b) **Other Sources:** Abandonment of Upland settlement in Southern Scotland - Martin L Parry. Agrarian Changes in South West Scotland. - Ian Whyte; Agrarian Landscape Terms - I H Adams; Agriculture and Society in Seventeenth Century Scotland - Ian Whyte; General View of the Agriculture of Ayr. - Aiton; The Drove Roads of Scotland - A R B Haldane; Economics of Scotland under the Commonwealth and the Protectorate - George Chalmers; Machinery on Farms - Thos Hutchison; Scotland from 11th Century to 1603 - Bruce Webster; Scottish Agriculture before the Improvers - T C Smout and Alexander Fenton; Scottish Farming, Past and Present - J A Symon; Scottish Country Life - Alexander Fenton.

2. **Fishing and Boat Building**

a) **National Records:-** Registers of Fishing Boats at Fishery Office, Ayr, and at Customs House, Greenock; Scottish Statistical Tables 1949, 1952 and 1975.

b) **Other Sources:-** Abstracts of Protocols of the Town Clerks of Glasgow - Renwick; Annals of Scotland; A View of the British Empire, more especially Scotland - with proposals for improvement of that Country - John Knox, 1785; The Boat House at Culzean - D Burrell; Brisbane Muniment Collection in Mitchell Library; The Fishing Industries of Scotland (1790 - 1914) - Malcolm Gray; Fifes of Fairlie - Ian McAllister (Wooden Boat 1989); William Fife and Son, The Birth of a Dynasty - John Leather (Classic Boat); Herrings and the Herring Fisheries - James Travis Jenkins; Fish Handling and Processing - Tory Research Station, Aberdeen; Glasgow Memorials - Robt. Renwick; Greenock Fish Sales Journal 1811 (Strathclyde Regional Archives); The Kist (Natural History and Antiquarian Society of Mid Argyll; Northern Scotland (A Historical Journal) 1972; Scottish Sailing Fishermen - R Hallewell; Scottish Salt Industry (1570-1850) - C A Whatley; Sailing Drifters - Edgar J March; Twelve Month and a Day - Chris. Rush.

3. **Textiles**
Ayrshire and other Whitework - M Swain; Chambers Guide to Traditional Crafts of Scotland - Carter and Rae; Fulling Mills - R A Pelham; Linen Hand Spinning and Weaving - P Baines; The Linen Trade - A J Warden; Scottish Linen Industry in the 18th Century - A Durie; Water Power in Scotland - I Shaw; Unpublished Ph D Thesis by Brenda Gaskin on Decline of the Hand Loom Weaving Industry in Scotland During the Years 1815-1845 (Edinburgh University 1955).

4. **Railways**
Glasgow & So West - Newsletters No 66 and No 75; Largs and Millport Weekly News, The Day the Train arrived in Largs; Railway Line to Largs Pier; Green Cars to Hurlford - Brian T Deans.

5. **General Trade**
Face of the Countryside in Central Ayrshire during eighteenth and nineteenth centuries - J H G Lebon; Old Maps and Rural Change in Ayrshire - J H G Lebon; Scottish Currency, Weights and Measures -Concise Scots Dictionary; Scottish Trade with Ireland in the 18th Century -L E Cochran; Scottish Trade on the Eve of the Union - T C Smout;